before and after the end of time architecture and the year 1000

CHRISTINE SMITH
with James Ackerman, Hunter Ford Tura,
Marco Steinberg, and Marjorie B. Cohn

before and after the end of time architecture and the year 1000

HARVARD DESIGN SCHOOL
in association with
GEORGE BRAZILLER, PUBLISHER

This is the first volume of a series of publications
related to the program MILLENNIUM MATTERS
sponsored by the Department of Architecture,
Harvard Design School

Front Cover:

Capital representing Samson destroying the House of the Philistines

Back Cover:

Corbel or metope representing a human face

This publication was produced by the Harvard Design School to accompany an exhibition at the Fogg Art Museum, Harvard University, August 26, 2000 to January 23, 2001.

ISBN 0-8076-1493-9

George Braziller, Inc.
171 Madison Avenue
New York, NY 10016

The Harvard Design School is a leading center for education, information, and technical expertise on the built environment. Its Departments of Architecture, Landscape Architecture, and Urban Planning and Design offer master's and doctoral degree programs and provide the foundation for the School's Advanced Studies and Executive Education programs.

Graphic Design: Matthew Monk, Providence, Rhode Island
Copyediting: Julia Collins, Somerville, Massachusetts
Production Coordination: Susan McNally, Cambridge, Massachusetts
Printing and Binding: Meridian Printing, East Greenwich, Rhode Island

Photography: Page xxii courtesy of the Pierpont Morgan Library; pages 5, 6, 8, 9, 10, 11, 12, 14, 15, 16, 18, 19, 21 David Matthews, Fogg Art Museum Photographic Services; pages 25, 36, 37, 39, 40, 41, 42, 42, 44, 45, 46, 47 Fogg Art Museum Photographic Services; pages 22, 31, 32, 33, 34, 35, 53, 55, 56, 57, 58, 59, 61, 62 Special Collections, Harvard University Graduate School of Design; pages 48, 49, 50, 51 Visual Collections, Fine Arts Library, Harvard University; pages 28, 52 Harvard University Archives; page 66 Steven Hutchison, Fogg Art Museum; pages 76, 78, 79, 80, 81, 82, 83, 84, 85, 86 Hillel Burger, Mineralogical Museum, Harvard University; pages 94, 96, 97 Steven Hutchison

contents

vii **preface** JORGE SILVETTI

xi **introduction** MARJORIE B. COHN AND CHRISTINE SMITH

xv **acknowledgments and list of lenders**

xvii **checklist of works exhibited**

essays

1 Before and After the End of Time CHRISTINE SMITH

29 The Human Architect and Architecture Made by Human Hands CHRISTINE SMITH

67 The Divine Architect and the Heavenly Jerusalem CHRISTINE SMITH

77 The Stones of the Heavenly Jerusalem HUNTER FORD TURA

89 Observations on Architectural Photography JAMES ACKERMAN

94 The Installation: A Question of Meaning and Representation MARCO STEINBERG

99 On the Study of Early Medieval Art at Harvard JAMES ACKERMAN

preface

MILLENNIUM MATTERS

"Millennium Matters" refers to a program of events, sponsored by the Department of Architecture at Harvard University's Graduate School of Design, that focuses on relationships among materials, ideas, and architecture, orchestrating a dialogue among history, technology, and design. Taking place during the academic year 2000/2001, the program comprises an exhibition at the Fogg Art Museum, commissioned installations at the GSD, a symposium, lectures, seminars, and design studios.

I regard this initiative as expressing the School's intense engagement of the richly complex conditions repositioning architecture among cultural and technical practices in contemporary society. Since theoretical discourse of architecture exists in a productive dialogue and complicity with the material specificity of buildings, I would suggest that the year-long program of events is rooted in sentiments, preoccupations, and events—a localized *zeitgeist*, if you will—that have defined the School's atmosphere in recent years. The GSD has traditionally engaged architecture with both modernity and the future, as manifested in recent initiatives exploring the promise of new technologies, as well as the expansion of the curriculum into allied disciplines and the Design Arts Initiative.

From my perspective, it is tempting to see awareness of the end of the millennium as provoking the convergence of heterogeneous ideas and energies at the Design School. Nevertheless, I would also characterize such a convergence as self-awareness, as the impulse was neither based on a need for celebration nor on a belief in the historical significance of the date, but rather on an acknowledgment of architecture's deeply rooted urges to imagine worlds that do not yet exist. Thus, instead of being a naïve response to social hype, the desire to acknowledge the millennium reflects a recognition of the inextricable, complex, and unique relationship that architecture has with the future. While most human activities deal with a future outcome, in my view, the task of physically representing the future state of society and culture, with any degree of totality, has fallen to architecture. Such efforts have not only powered the architectural imagination but also engendered profound moral stands. Buildings belong to a unique species of objects that establish *parahuman* relationships with time. For, although they are intended to outlast their creators, their physical realizations are separated from their conceptions by unusually long periods.

Not surprisingly, these obligations incite both excitement and apprehension, the latter reinforced by a well-rooted skepticism about architects' ability to predict the future that resulted from the postmodern unraveling of modernism's ideology and the exposure of the demagogic and autocratic foundations of its all-too-literal images of political utopias reified in future buildings and future cities. Nowadays, debunking the future, as envisioned by architects, is the norm. Since the 1960s, any idea of prediction or sense of "futurology" has become almost automatically suspect for architecture. Yet I believe that it remains an essential task for architects to look toward the future. Therefore, the idea of the GSD's acknowledging the millennium reconfirms our identity by recognizing one of architecture's unique potentials although, in the same moment, raising the problem of its dubious prophetic tendencies.

During the academic year 1997–1998, Professor Christine Smith proposed a pair of exhibitions contrasting the status of materials, technology, and the role of the architect at two millennial boundaries. The first exhibition, curated by Professor Smith together with Marjorie Cohn of the Fogg Art Museum and titled *Before and After the End of Time: Architecture and the Year 1000*—the subject of this publication—focuses on the turn of the first millennium and the revival of stone construction. The relevance of materials for future architects has always been clear to me, not only because of the technical and symbolic attributes of various stones but just as importantly for the significance of materiality in historical analysis. Further, the pairing of the year 1000 with a technical subject offered a model for our initiative by reinforcing important departmental pedagogical objectives, while dealing with the millennial shift in a *de facto*, critical manner that avoided the simplistic traps of prediction.

The theme of the second exhibition emerged with the decisive help of Professor Toshiko Mori. Titled *Before and After the Shift in Time*, it inquires into the potential effects that can be imagined or programmed by the use of new materials or the redeployment of well-known ones. Unlike Professor Smith's scholarly project, this second project will be both speculative and prospective in scope.

While the first exhibition seeks to interpret what did happen or could have happened around the year 1000, the second exhibition will explore what new materials suggest for the future of architecture. Professor Mori and her collaborators will do this through installations designed by GSD faculty members. Together, these two events concentrate on the theoretical and technical impact that materials have on design ideas and the design process. It is the focus on this obstinate attribute of architecture—"materiality"—that links the intellectual content of the two exhibitions. For materiality is more than a technical property of buildings: it is a precondition that promotes ideas, creativity, and pleasure in architecture, and it guides us to the loftiest aspirations of theory.

This two-part event, straddling the years 2000 and 2001, presents to the public the breadth of our academic endeavors in scholarship and artistic creativity. Comparisons between the two exhibitions, the two historical periods, and the two modes of inquiry are inevitable and I hope that the richness of the exhibition will provoke viewers' imaginations and critical abilities while suggesting new ways for architecture to address the future. To this end, the School has embraced, however briefly, the fiction that the millennium indeed matters.

JORGE SILVETTI
Nelson Robinson, Jr., Professor of Architecture
Chair, Department of Architecture
Graduate School of Design

introduction

This exhibition contrasts the architecture that might have come into being in the year 1000, that is, the Heavenly Jerusalem, with the architecture that did appear, the Romanesque. Had the world ended, as many believed was prophesied in the biblical Apocalypse of John, all of creation including time would have been replaced by a new city made by God. However, the world didn't end in the year 1000. Instead, one of the most fecund periods in the history of architecture, the Romanesque, began. Central to this new architecture was the revival of cut-stone masonry, which had fallen into disuse for almost half of the preceding millennium. Revival of stone use in building at once presupposed and stimulated technology, for stone has to be quarried, transported, and lifted into place—all operations requiring skilled labor, mechanical devices, and specialized tools. Thus the year 1000 marks the upsurge of a technological revolution.

The revival of stone masonry had an equally important impact on design, especially in the engineering of walls and vaults but also in the sculptural treatment of the wall masses or other manipulations of the mural boundary for aesthetic effect. The fruit of this exploration matured over the next seven hundred years, perhaps attaining its highest development in the architecture of the eighteenth century. Although the Heavenly Jerusalem did not descend in the year 1000, a new era did, nonetheless, begin.

"Millennium" is from the Latin word for "one thousand" and defines a period of one thousand years. Since time is calculated by a calendar, it follows that the measurement of the millennium is culturally determined by which calendar is in use. This exhibition is concerned with western medieval culture that inherited from Julius Caesar the determination that a year comprised 365 days with a leap year of 366 days every fourth year (the Julian calendar); and from the sixth-century monk Dionysius Exiguus the decision that the Christian era (*anno Domini*) began with Jesus Christ's incarnation in A.D. 1. This calendar is as much a cultural construct as a means of measurement, differing, for instance, from that of ancient Rome, which counted historical time from the date of the foundation of Rome (21 April, 753 B.C.) as well as from the calendars of other, contemporary cultures such as Islam, which counts from 16 July A.D. 622, and Byzantium, where time was counted from the creation of the world in 5508 B.C.

From a scientific standpoint, the western European calendar has some fundamental problems. For instance, since Dionysius didn't allow for a year zero it isn't clear whether the year 1000 in fact corresponded to the end of the first or beginning of the second millennium. And, since Jesus was born before

4 B.C., a more accurate calculation of time elapsed since the Incarnation would place the end of the first millennium in 996 or earlier. Association of the year 1000 with the turn of the millennium, therefore, is conventional and approximate rather than scientifically or historically precise. Nonetheless, the calendar that establishes the current year as A.D. 2000 remains (except for some reforms by Pope Gregory XIII in 1582) the same used in western Europe a thousand years ago; therefore the organizers have followed it in planning this exhibition.

The predictions that many believed would be fulfilled at the end of the first millennium are chiefly recounted in the Apocalypse of John: the end of time and of the created world, the Last Judgment, and the beginning of a new, eternal epoch. In other words, the year 1000 could have marked the climactic end of both historical and spiritual time. The central themes of this exhibition are the intersection and divergence of these two kinds of time and the parallel metaphor of the two cities, the earthly and the Heavenly Jerusalem. These themes juxtapose the City of God with the City of Man, the eternal with the temporal, and the divine with the human architect. Not only the selection of works but also the physical ordering of their display articulates these concepts. Thus, an imaginary tour of the exhibition will introduce the reader to its content.

The exhibition contrasts what might have happened in the year 1000 with what did happen as exemplified by architecture. Visualizations of the end of time, displayed on the end wall of the exhibition, confront the visitor entering the gallery: a series of lithographs by Odilon Redon and a lost tympanum from Cluny III, reconstructed by Kenneth J. Conant, depict the events of the Apocalypse. Some sense of the Romanesque style is conveyed by drawings, photographs, and sculptures in the vestibule of the gallery and on its entrance wall.

The contrast between human and divine architecture is exemplified by works placed on the opposing side walls of the Fogg's Lehmann Gallery. The right wall depicts the Heavenly Jerusalem, in a rendering abstracted from a tenth-century manuscript illumination. The city's walls are made of precious and semiprecious stones embedded in gold. On the opposite wall, examples of Romanesque carvings are displayed on mounts that evoke their original architectural context. Thus gemstones, the building blocks of the divine architect, are juxtaposed with limestone and marble worked by human hands: the installation supplies their respective architectural contexts, enabling the spectator to imagine the whole architectural structure while examining in detail their constituent elements.

Early on, the organizers chose to create the exhibition from materials in Harvard University collections and from works not usually on view. The Harvard Art Museums have substantial holdings apart from those familiar to the public through exhibition, as is only appropriate in a teaching museum, where so-called "study materials" offer instructive comparisons for problems in technical analysis, attribution, dating, function, and cultural context. Among these study materials are objects collected or identified as worthy of acquisition by generations of Harvard faculty members whose research was furthered by archeological campaigns in the field. Although today this tradition survives in the Fogg Art Museum's formal participation in the archeological exploration of Sardis, the ancient kingdom in modern Turkey, formerly the excavation of Romanesque Latin Europe (the area now divided among France, Italy, Germany, and Spain) was also a Harvard professorial specialty.

Traditionally, the Fogg's public display of Romanesque material has been largely restricted to a magnificent set of twelfth-century Burgundian capitals, which are large enough to be integrated into the building's walls, around the Warburg Hall or in the ambulatory of the museum courtyard. Only occasionally have other objects, such as the apostle column featured in this exhibition, found a place on view. To be sure, the museum has almost since its opening been constrained for space; but more pertinently, in the case of the Romanesque material included in *Before and After the End of Time*, the Fogg through most of its history has been a museum of fine art. Stone carving that could not sustain viewing as stone sculpture, because of fragmentary condition or formlessness in isolation from an original architectural context, has not generally been considered "exhibition-worthy."

The Fogg Art Museum has recently, however, extended its mandate to architecture and design, establishing in 1999 a formal curatorial department with an affiliation with the Graduate School of Design. Once criteria for an exhibition based in architecture were framed more narrowly within an iconographical and historiographical context, rather than aesthetic and art historical, a rich lode of potential exhibition objects was revealed within the Fogg Art Museum; at institutions in its nearby academic vicinity, such as the Fine Arts Library and the Frances Loeb Library of the Graduate School of Design; and even at the unexpected remove of the Mineralogical Collection of the Museum of Natural History.

It has been possible to present more than sixty objects that meet our basic criteria of presence at Harvard and absence from regular exhibition. Hence a subtheme to the exhibition became the study of medieval art at Harvard, a theme that we developed in selecting portraits of major figures involved in the study of Romanesque art and architecture. To further highlight this theme, drawings and photographs collected or made by each of these protagonists are grouped together.

The exhibition also addresses the difficult problem of how to mount a show on monumental architecture within a museum setting. Discovering means of conveying a proper sense of scale is the obvious problem. Since no examples of eleventh-century architecture are accessible in the United States and the Heavenly Jerusalem is—at least at this point in time—only imagined on the basis of literary texts, we also sought ways of providing some sense of architectural context, materiality, and visual effect. For this reason, the installation itself is integral to the concept of the exhibition and is illustrated in this publication.

Before and After the End of Time: Architecture and the Year 1000 brings to life some of the most powerful, enduring, and influential ideas in the western European cultural tradition and in Christian theology. Furthermore, it brings before the spectator architectural monuments from a period with which few are familiar. Finally, it focuses the meaning of the year 2000 by illustrating its historical and cultural tradition.

MARJORIE B. COHN
Carl A. Weyerhaeuser Curator of Prints
Fogg Art Museum

CHRISTINE SMITH
Robert C. and Marion K. Weinberg Professor of Architectural History
Graduate School of Design

December 31, 1999

acknowledgments and list of lenders

The organizers thank The Samuel Kress Foundation for its generous support of this publication. The Gladys Kreble Delmas Foundation made possible the unusual installation; other funding was provided by the Graduate School of Design and the Fogg Art Museum.

We wish to thank Ivan Gaskell, Margaret S. Winthrop Curator, and Sarah B. Kianovsky, assistant curator, paintings, sculpture and decorative art, and Amanda Ricker-Prugh, assistant registrar, all of the Fogg Art Museum for their essential assistance in making the collection of Romanesque sculpture accessible for study and exhibition. We also thank Henry Lie, Danielle Hanrahan, Evelyn Rosenthal, and the staff members of their departments who have contributed so greatly to the realization of our conception. We are grateful to Caleb Smith of the visual collections, Fine Arts Library, for access to the A. K. Porter photographs; to Mary Daniels, librarian and curator of special collections, Frances Loeb Library, Graduate School of Design, for lending the Kenneth J. Conant and H. H. Richardson materials; to Ann Whiteside, curator of visual resources, Graduate School of Design, for permission to reproduce the portrait photo of Conant; to Harley Holden, curator of the University Archives, for permission to reproduce the portrait photos of H. H. Richardson and A. K. Porter; to the Pierpont Morgan Library for permission to use the Morgan Beatus Heavenly Jerusalem as the template for our installation and Eva Soos for her assistance in expediting our request; to Carl A. Francis, curator of the Mineralogical Museum, Museum of Natural History, for the loan of gemstones; and to the House of Onyx, Inc. for the loan of jasper, sardonyx, and chalcedony samples.

checklist of works exhibited

NOTE: References in the text and captions are to the checklist.

1. **The Heavenly Jerusalem**
Folio 22 v from *Commentary on the Apocalypse*
by Beatus of Liébana, Spanish
ca. 940–945, written by Maius at
the Monastery of San Miguel de Escalada
Photographic reproduction
Courtesy of the Pierpont Morgan Library,
New York (mss. 644)
TL37103.1

Numbers 2–13
Odilon Redon
French, 1840–1916
Twelve plates from the *Apocalypse de Saint Jean*, 1899
Lithograph, 22 1/4 x 16 5/8 (sheet) inches
Fogg Art Museum, Gift of Philip Hofer
M4257–M4268

2. Titled: "...et il avait dans sa main droite sept étoiles, et de sa bouche sortait une épée aigue à deux tranchants" ("and he had in his right hand seven stars and from his mouth came a sharp sword, double edged"). Apoc. 1:16

NOTE: The English versions are not translations but are the equivalent passage in the Jerusalem Bible.

3. Titled: "...Puis je vis, dans la main droite de celui qui était assis sur la trône, un livre écrit dedans et dehors, scellé de sept sceaux" ("And I saw that in the right hand of the One sitting on the throne there was a scroll that had writing on back and front and was sealed with seven seals"). Apoc. 5:1

4. Titled: "...et celui qui était monté dessus se nommait la Mort" ("and his name that sat on him was Death"). Apoc. 6:8

5. Titled: "Puis l'ange prit l'encensoir" ("Then the angel took the censer"). Apoc. 8:5

6. Titled: "et il tombe du ciel une grande étoile ardente comme un flambeau" ("and I saw a star that had fallen from heaven on to the earth"). Apoc. 9:1

7. Titled: "...une femme revêtue du Soleil" ("a woman clothed with the Sun"). Apoc. 12:1

8. Titled: "Et un autre ange sortit du temple qui est au ciel, ayant lui aussi une faucille tranchante" ("Another angel, who also carried a sharp sickle, came out of the temple in heaven"). Apoc. 14:17

9. Titled: "Après cela je vis descendre du ciel un ange qui avait la clef de l'abîme et une grande chaîne en sa main" ("Then I saw an angel come down from heaven with the key of the abyss in his hand and an enormous chain"). Apoc. 20:1

10. Titled: "...et le lia pour mille ans" ("and chained him up for a thousand years"). Apoc. 20:2

11. Titled: "...et le diable qui les séduisait, fut jeté dans l'étang de feu et de soufre, où est la bête et le faux prophète" ("then the devil, who misled them, will be thrown into the lake of fire and sulphur, where the beast and the false prophet are"). Apoc. 20:10

12. Titled: "Et moi, Jean, je vis la sainte cité, la nouvelle Jérusalem, qui descendait du Ciel d'auprès de Dieu" ("I saw the holy city, and the new Jerusalem, coming down from God out of Heaven"). Apoc. 21:2

13. Titled: "C'est moi, Jean, qui ai vu et qui ai ouï ces choses" ("I, John, am the one who heard and saw these things"). Apoc. 22:8

14. Spanish, from Santa Maria de Lebanza (Palencia)
Capital: front face, **Christ in Majesty with Symbols of the Evangelists**; left and right sides,
Apostles with Instruments of the Passion
1185–1190
Limestone, 25 x 24 (top) x 15 inches
Fogg Art Museum, Friends of the Fogg Art Museum
1926.4.1A

15. Kenneth John Conant
American, 1894–1984
Tympanum of Cluny III
Colored pencil, 37 x 29 inches
Graduate School of Design, Special Collections
Cluny Collection
TL37104.1

16. French, from St.-Pons-de-Thomières, Herault
Capital: left side, **The City of Emmaus**;
principal face, **The Supper at Emmaus**;
other long face, **The Journey to Emmaus**;
right side, **Noli me tangere**
ca. 1140
Marble, 15 x 20 (top) x 13 inches
Fogg Art Museum,
Gift of Arthur Kingsley Porter
1922.67

17. **Portrait of Henry Hobson Richardson**
(by George Collins Cox ?)
Photograph, modern print
Harvard University Archives
HUP Richardson, Henry Hobson, A.B. 1859 (3)
TL37103.2

18. **San Michele in Pavia, Interior**, 12th c.
Photograph, 10 1/2 x 15 inches
Graduate School of Design, Special Collections
Richardson Collection (no. 301–33)
TL37104.2

19. **San Zeno in Verona, Exterior**, 11th and 12th c.
Photograph, 12 1/4 x 9 7/8 inches
Graduate School of Design, Special Collections
Richardson Collection (no. 301–35)
TL37104.3

20. **Abbaye des Dames in Caen, Exterior, West Façade**, 11th c.
Photograph, 11 x 8 1/2 inches
Graduate School of Design, Special Collections
Richardson Collection (no. 28116–12)
TL37104.4

21. **St. Gereon in Cologne, Exterior from East**, 11th to 13th c.
Photograph, 7 3/4 x 6 1/4 inches
Graduate School of Design, Special Collections
Richardson Collection (no. 21817–27)
TL37104.5

22. **Cathedral in Trier, Exterior from the East**, 11th and 12th c.
Photograph, 6 x 4 inches
Graduate School of Design, Special Collections
Richardson Collection (no. 21817–17)
TL37104.6

23. French, from Cluny
Architectural Frieze, Representing Two Arcaded Structures
second quarter of the 12th c.
Limestone, 9 x 15 inches
Fogg Art Museum, Alpheus Hyatt Fund
1949.47.94

24. French, from Cluny?
Fragment of a Capital for an Engaged Column
ca. 1125
Limestone, 8 1/2 x 10 x 8 1/2 inches
Fogg Art Museum, Alpheus Hyatt Fund
1949.47.92

25. French, from Burgundy
Corbel, Representing a Crouching Human Figure
ca. 1150
Limestone, 11 x 7 x 10 inches
Fogg Art Museum, Alpheus Hyatt Fund
1949.47.29

26. French, from Burgundy
Corbel, Representing a Crouching Human Figure
ca. 1150
Limestone, 11 x 7 1/2 x 14 1/2 inches
Fogg Art Museum, Alpheus Hyatt Fund
1949.47.30

27. Western France
Corbel or Metope Representing a Human Face
ca. 1125
Limestone, 8 1/2 inches
Fogg Art Museum, Alpheus Hyatt Fund
1949.47.61

28. French, from Notre-Dame-des-Doms, Avignon
Capital: left side, **Samson Destroying the House of the Philistines**;
main face, **Samson Wrestling with the Lion**;
rear face, **Delilah Cutting Samson's Hair and**
Samson Captured by the Philistines;
right side, **Samson Carrying off the Gates of Gaza**
third quarter of the 12th c.
Marble, 12 1/2 x 10 1/2 (top) inches
Fogg Art Museum, Gift of Meta and Paul J. Sachs
1922.32

29. Spanish, from the Monastery of San Pelayo Antealtares, Santiago de Compostela
Columnar Support with Three Apostles: Matthias, Jude, and Simon
1125–1150
Marble, 45 3/4 x 7 (top) inches
Fogg Art Museum, Gift of the Republic of Spain through the Museo Arqueologico Nacional and Arthur Kingsley Porter
1933.100

30. French, from Burgundy or Champagne
Capital with Acanthus Leaves
third quarter of the 12th c.
Limestone, 30 1/4 x 30 (top) x 16 1/2 inches
Fogg Art Museum, Alpheus Hyatt Fund
1949.47.125

31. French, from the Abbey of Dommartin, Pas-de-Calais
Fragment of a Capital
ca. 1160
Limestone, 9 1/2 x 10 1/2 inches
Fogg Art Museum, Alpheus Hyatt Fund
1949.47.27

32. French, from eastern France
Abacus with Rinceau of Leaves and Beaded Interlace
last quarter of the 12th c.
Limestone, 7 1/2 x 20 x 13 inches
Fogg Art Museum, Alpheus Hyatt Fund
1949.47.134

33. Spanish, from north central Spain
Corbel Representing a Cow
mid 12th c.
Limestone, 9 x 10 x 21 inches
Fogg Art Museum, Alpheus Hyatt Fund
1949.47.153

34. French, from La Madeleine, Vézelay
Spandrel with a Saint, Hind, and Hunter
second quarter of the 12th c.
Limestone, 15 1/2 x 31 x 5 1/2 inches
Fogg Art Museum, Alpheus Hyatt Fund
1949.47.70

35. French, from La Madeleine, Vézelay
Spandrel with a Wreath of Leaves Enclosing Pinecones
second quarter of the 12th c.
Limestone, 9 1/2 x 14 1/2 x 4 1/2 inches
Fogg Art Museum, Alpheus Hyatt Fund
1949.47.146

36. Arthur Kingsley Porter
American, 1883–1933
Tomb of Abbot Isarne (d. 1048), Marseilles, St.-Victoire
Photograph, modern print
Fine Arts Library, Visual Collections (neg. #1180)
TL37105.2

37. Arthur Kingsley Porter
American, 1883–1933
Gospel Book, Vich, Episcopal Museum (mss. 89)
Photograph, modern print
Fine Arts Library, Visual Collections (neg. #288L)
TL37105.2

38. Arthur Kingsley Porter
American, 1883–1933
Capital with Apostles and Symbol of St. Luke
French, 11th c.
Photograph, modern print
Fine Arts Library, Visual Collections (neg. #924A)
TL37105.3

39. Arthur Kingsley Porter
American, 1883–1933
Reliquary of St. John the Baptist, Detail of St. Peter
Spanish, ivory, 11th c.
Photograph, modern print
Fine Arts Library, Visual Collections (neg. #6068)
TL37105.4

40. Arthur Kingsley Porter
American, 1883–1933
South Cross, East Face, Castledermot, County Kildare
Photograph, 6 5/8 x 4 3/4 inches
Fine Arts Library, Visual Collections (neg. #6928)
TL37105.5

41. **Arthur Kingsley Porter and Lucy Porter in Their Car**
Photograph, modern print
Harvard University Archives, HUG 1706.125 p Box 1
TL37103.3

42. **Portrait of Kenneth J. Conant in an Excavation Trench at Cluny, 1931**
Photograph, modern print from a lantern slide
Graduate School of Design, Visual Resources
(Lantern B 398/x19)
TL37103.4

43. Kenneth J. Conant
American, 1894–1984
Cluny II from West
Pencil, 14 x 14 1/2 inches
Graduate School of Design, Special Collections
Cluny Collection
TL37104.7

44. Kenneth J. Conant
American, 1894–1984
View of Cluny III from East, with Partial Plan Attached
Colored pencil, 37 x 25 inches
Graduate School of Design, Special Collections
Cluny Collection
TL37104.8

45. Kenneth J. Conant
American, 1894–1984
Perspective View of Interior of Cluny III
Mixed media, 13 x 9 1/2 inches
Graduate School of Design, Special Collections
Cluny Collection
TL37104.9

46. Kenneth J. Conant
American, 1894–1984
Kenneth J. Conant with His Installation of the Apse of Cluny in the Fogg Museum Courtyard, 1934
Photographic collage, 9 3/4 x 7 1/2 inches
Graduate School of Design, Visual Resources
(Lantern B398/h22 Cluny, 1934)
TL37104.10

47. Kenneth J. Conant
American, 1894–1984
Plan, Apse of Cluny III
pencil, 48 x 28 inches
Graduate School of Design, Special Collections,
Cluny Collection
TL37104.11

48. Kenneth J. Conant
American, 1894–1984
Capital from Cluny III
Collage of photograph, black ink, and pencil
14 3/4 x 9 3/8 inches
Graduate School of Design, Special Collections
Cluny Collection
TL37104.12

49. Kenneth J. Conant
American, 1894–1984
Cluny Superimposed on the Town of Cluny
Collage of photograph, black ink, and pencil
11 x 15 inches
Graduate School of Design, Special Collections
Cluny Collection
TL37104.13

50. **Drawing abstracting the geometry of the Morgan Beatus Heavenly Jerusalem.**
The twelve gemstones are represented by photographic details of rough-cut samples. Identification starting at top left follows with checklist numbers 52–63.

51. The same twelve gemstones used in the same order as checklist number 50, showing polished and faceted samples.

52–63 The twelve stones of the Heavenly Jerusalem
Jasper
Lapis lazuli
Chalcedony
Emerald
Sardonyx
Sard (Carnelian)
Chrysolite (Peridot)
Beryl (Aquamarine)
Topaz
Chrysoprase
Jacinth
Amethyst
The jasper, chalcedony, and sardonyx are on exhibition courtesy of House of Onyx, Greenville, KY (TL 37099.4,6,2,3). The remaining stones have been loaned by the Mineralogical Museum, Harvard University (TL 37321.1–8). The illustrations are taken from rough-cut samples in the Mineralogical Museum.

NOTE: dimensions are in inches, height before width before depth (where applicable)
Numbers 14, 23, 30, and 35 were not in the exhibition.

essays

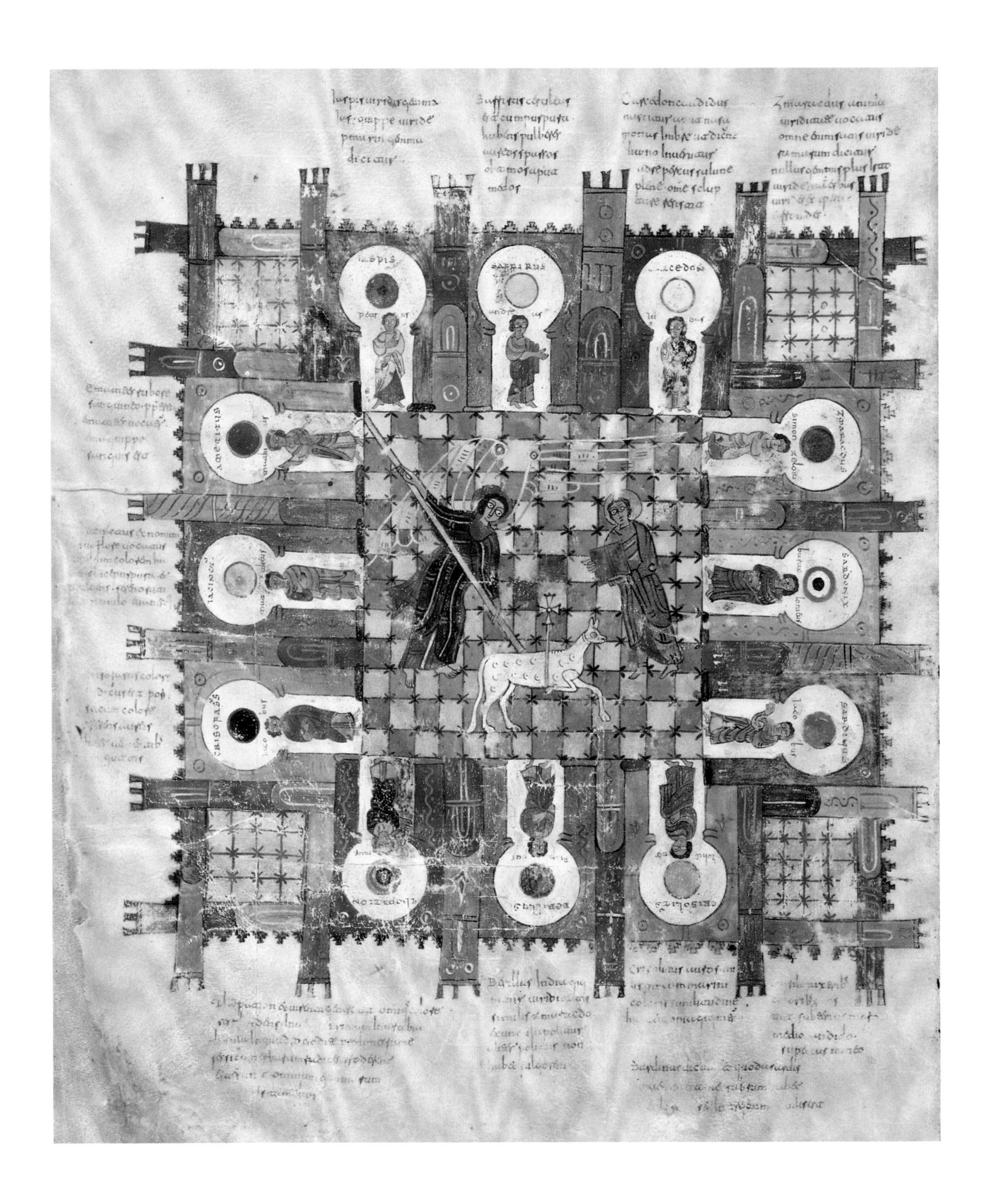

1 The Heavenly Jerusalem from the Morgan Beatus

before and after the end of time

CHRISTINE SMITH

We read in the Old Testament that the events that would accompany the end of the world were revealed in a vision to the prophet Daniel in the time of Cyrus, King of Persia. Daniel asked: "how long until these wonders take place?" (Dan. 12:6). Prophecy about when—and how—the world will end is an important theme in the Judeo-Christian tradition on which medieval culture in western Europe was largely built. Indeed, the belief that the world was created by a supreme deity from nothing and that it would end distinguished Christian thought from that of the most authoritative classical philosophers. Although Plato believed the world to have been created, he did not think it was destructible; for Aristotle, the world was both uncreated and indestructible. These pagan views were rejected in the Middle Ages in favor of the Christian understanding, based on Scripture, that the world was created and will end. The dominant culture in the time and place the exhibition is concerned with—western Europe in the centuries around A.D. 1000—was Christian, and it is within that culture that we will explore the idea of the millennium.

Daniel's question "how long" expressed his belief in the importance of measurement and duration. The Old Testament takes time very seriously, stating the duration of important happenings: God created the world in six days and rested on the seventh (Gen. 1–2:3); during the Great Flood it rained for forty days and forty nights (Gen. 7:17); Solomon built the Temple in Jerusalem in twenty years (2 Chron. 8:1). But the angel's answer to Daniel's question about when the world would end was enigmatic rather than precise: "A time and two times, and half a time." Daniel commented that although he listened, he couldn't understand what the angel said.

The Jesus of the New Testament was often precise about time, fasting in the wilderness for forty days (Luke 4:2), foretelling that he would be raised from the dead on the third day (Luke 9:22). He also spoke about the end of time, an event that he associated with the end of the world and the coming of the timeless eternity of God's kingdom. Although Jesus suggested that this would occur within the lifetime of his followers (Matt. 16:24–28; Mark 1, 13:30, 14:62), he also said that "as for that day and hour, nobody knows it" (Matt. 24:36). In the Bible, Jesus often spoke in ways that could be interpreted on different levels, literal and spiritual. This second level of meaning was embedded in metaphors, parables, and paradoxical sayings. When he spoke, therefore, of the Kingdom of God as being near, or even present, he did not necessarily mean that the world was about to end. Ambiguity about how the temporal frame of reference within which Jesus' sayings, as preserved in the four Gospels, should be understood gave rise to diverse understandings of the millennium in the Middle Ages.

Two very different notions of time had equal currency around the year 1000. One, determined by the calendar and measuring historical time, understood the end of the millennium to coincide with the year 1000. The other understood that this kind of time is a human convention and that God's millennium is entirely different. St. Peter drew on the poetic suggestion in the Old Testament—"for a thousand years in your sight are but as yesterday when it is past" (Ps. 89:4)—to warn the earliest Christians that no one can know when the world will end because “with the Lord, ‘a day’ can mean a thousand years, and a thousand years is like a day” (2 Pet. 3:8). From the point of view of eternity, the millennium is not a date but an event in the history of human salvation. Thus St. Paul’s evocation of the beatific vision—“for now we see as in a mirror dimly, but then face to face” (1 Cor. 13:12)—was understood in the period that concerns us not only as historical prophecy, but also as a measure of spiritual enlightenment. A central theme of this exhibition is the intersection and divergence of historical and spiritual time, both centered on the idea of the millennium.

Paul’s summary of Jesus’ teaching about the end of time in his letter to the Corinthians explained that Jesus would return (the Second Coming), defeat his enemies, including death itself, and then turn over the Kingdom to God the Father (1 Cor. 15:20–34). Paul distinguished between the temporally limited life of the perishable body and the eternal life of the spirit: “we are not all going to die, but we shall all be changed.”

The association between the end of the world and the millennium is most clearly brought out in the Apocalypse of John, written about fifty years after Jesus died. “Apocalypse” is the Greek word for “disclosure” and the work is also called the Book of Revelation. It recounts a complex vision revealed to St. John by an angel on the island of Patmos around A.D. 85. It is in the Apocalypse that the millennium is explicitly associated with the end of the world (Apoc. 20:1–6). However, this short passage describing the thousand-year reign of Christ and the saints, prelude to the end of the world, the Last Judgment, and the coming of the Kingdom of God, presents special interpretive problems. It is by no means clear how the temporal framework of the visions corresponds to that of human history. Most crucially, if the thousand-year reign of Christ began with his Incarnation (theoretically in the year zero), then the year 1000 would mark the end of the millennium and therefore the end of time, the Last Judgment, and the advent of the Kingdom of God. But if the millennium begins with the Second Coming of Christ, then this could occur in the year 1000 or at any time. The significance of the year 1000 (the chronological millennium), in other words, depends on its relation to the thousand-year reign of Christ (the theological millennium).

Until about A.D. 400 John’s detailed narrative of the end of time and the coming of the Heavenly Kingdom was understood as predicting factual events that had taken, or would take, place. For the persecuted Christian Church of the first three centuries of the common era, it could only predict a future triumph; for John, the thousand-year reign had clearly not yet begun. But after the conversion to Christianity of the Emperor Constantine in A.D. 312 and the subsequent conversion of much of the Roman Empire, this interpretation was less satisfactory. With the closing of pagan temples in the late fourth century, the triumph of the Church seemed (at least to those in the center of the empire) complete. Beginning with the commentary on the Apocalypse by Tyconius (ca. 385), the millennium began to be interpreted as a spiritual and moralizing allegory of the present reign of Christ embodied in the Church and of the struggle between good and evil until the Second Coming and the advent of the Heavenly Kingdom. In this view, the Second Coming would end, rather than initiate, the millennium. St. Augustine, for instance, taught that Pentecost (the descent of the Holy Spirit after Jesus’ Ascension) marked the beginning of the thousand-year reign (*City of God* 20:7–9).

The commentary on the Apocalypse by Beatus of Liébana, an Asturian monk who in 786 compiled the main previous interpretations of John's revelations into an encyclopedic survey, exemplifies this theological approach. For him, the reign began with the Incarnation and corresponds to the sixth, and last, day of creation. According to Beatus' calculation, the sixth millennium would end in the year 1000, and the world would end in the sixth millennium. However, it did not follow, for him, that the world would end in the year 1000, since God might either extend or cut short the sixth millennium and because terms such as "day" do not always signify temporal units. Rather, understood symbolically, the message to be gleaned is that the day of resurrection will come in the sixth millennium, although we can't know its time, or year or day. Nonetheless, Beatus suggested that the world would end sometime during the year 1000. This type of exegesis changed again with the work of Rupert of Deutz (1075/80–1129) and Joachim of Flore (1130–1202), returning to a historical–prophetic interpretation and drawing connections between the visions and specific persons and events.

It isn't clear, therefore, whether people living in the centuries that concern us understood themselves to be living before, during, or after the thousand-year reign of Christ, either temporally or spiritually. Yet those who followed Augustine and Beatus (presumably the majority of educated people) must have believed themselves to be alive during the millennial reign of Christ, somewhere near the end of the sixth and last age of the world.

THE APOCALYPSE

The events narrated in the Apocalypse were illustrated as a pictorial cycle as early as the fifth century in a lost manuscript that is the prototype for a number of tenth-century and later works. Especially prominent in this pictorial tradition are illustrations accompanying the commentary of Beatus: the central image of the Heavenly Jerusalem in our exhibition is taken from a mid-tenth-century Spanish Beatus manuscript (one of twenty-four surviving Beatus exemplars), now in the Pierpont Morgan Library in New York (number 1). We will examine the Morgan Beatus more closely in a later chapter. Our concern here is to review the events of the Apocalypse, which in our exhibition are illustrated primarily in a series of lithographs by the nineteenth-century artist Odilon Redon.

The Redon *Apocalypse de Saint Jean* series (numbers 2–13), comprising twelve lithographs first published in 1899, seemed an especially appropriate choice for this exhibition. This series is in great contrast to the more famous Apocalypse series by Albrecht Dürer, also available in the Fogg Art Museum collection. Yet Dürer's powerful conceptualization of the narrative is so detailed it would give a false specificity to our evocation of the actual millennium of A.D. 1000; and its late Gothic style—it was published as a series in 1498—while as far removed from that date as from ours appears to modern eyes as archaic as the Romanesque, falsifying its actual aesthetic distance. The lithographs by Redon, manifestly more subjective and less filled with incident as well as closer to our own times, provide a more transparent window into an eternal moment. Redon himself was a lapsed Catholic and although biblical subjects appear frequently in his work after 1894 (he died in 1916), this series does not have a strongly theological character. Indeed, although it could be described as literary (all of the lithographs include quotations from the Apocalypse) it could not be described as learned. The series does not embody medieval theological ideas but is sufficiently neutral in this regard to harmonize with the content of works produced closer in time to the year 1000 in the exhibition. Redon's artistic personality, always focused on imagination, on fantasy and the ambiguous, was well suited to the illustration of John's visions. His apocalyptic prints serve admirably to evoke the drama, often human, of the text and to illustrate its main events.

Redon said that "suggestive art cannot give anything without exclusive recourse to the mysterious play of shadows and to the rhythm of mentally conceived lines." His lithographs depend entirely on chiaroscuro, the contrast of light and dark, reflecting the strong impact made on the artist by his study of Rembrandt. Redon saw Rembrandt's chiaroscuro as the secret of his predecessor's whole work, "a completely picturesque invention which incarnates the idea and gives it flesh and bones, so to speak." This aptly describes the effect of Redon's *Apocalypse de Saint Jean* series as well.

Our concern, however, is less with Redon's artistry than with the Christian notion of the millennium, above all as found in John's revelations. It will be most useful, then, to outline the events of the Apocalypse, commenting on their significance in the year 1000 as well as on their representation in the works presented here.

THE LETTERS TO THE SEVEN CHURCHES

Most of the first three chapters of the Apocalypse concerns letters John was instructed to send by Jesus, who appeared to him as eschatological judge, to seven churches in Asia (Ephesus, Smyrna, Pergamum, Thyatira, Sardis, Philadelphia, and Laodicea). Redon illustrates this initial vision quite literally with the figure of a man with a double-edged sword protruding from his mouth, his face shining like the sun, and seven stars (the seven churches) in his right hand (number 2).

2 Odilon Redon: ***Apocalypse de Saint Jean*** **Apoc. 1:16**

6

3 Apoc. 5:1

THE SEVEN SEALS

Redon's next print illustrates the opening of chapter 5, the vision of God holding a scroll sealed with seven seals (number 3). Only the Lamb, understood in our period to symbolize Jesus, would be able to break these. The image includes three of the four winged creatures surrounding the throne (the lion, the eagle, and the bull) but omits the human being. Also omitted are the elders on thrones referred to in the opening of chapter 4. Thus Redon's image includes some, but not all, of the iconographic elements that identify the *Maiestas Domini* (Majesty of the Lord), so frequently represented in our period. We will return to this subject in greater detail below. Chapters 5 through 7 recount what happened as the first six seals were opened. The first four seals released four horsemen: Victory, War, Famine, and Death. Redon illustrated this last with a skeleton, mounted on a horse, holding a long sharp sword (number 4). The fifth seal released the vengeance of the martyrs. With the sixth, the sun went black, the moon turned red as blood, the stars fell from the sky, and the sky rolled up like a scroll, while all on earth cried out in fear because the day of judgment had arrived.

When the Lamb broke the seventh seal, there was silence in heaven "for about half an hour." This is the opening of the eighth chapter. Then an angel took a censer filled with fire from the prayers of the saints and flung it down on earth. Redon depicted a beautiful woman as the angel, with feathered wings, holding a censer from which immense clouds of incense pour out (number 5).

THE SEVEN TRUMPETS

The angels then sounded their trumpets and great destruction fell on earth. As the fifth angel blew his trumpet (beginning of chapter 9) John saw a star that had fallen from heaven. Although this refers to the fallen angel Lucifer, whose name means "bearer of light," Redon chose a literal depiction—a ball of light—rather than an interpretive one (number 6). Lucifer opened the abyss, which emitted great clouds of smoke that became swarms of locusts, which stung like scorpions. They were told to attack those who did not have God's seal on their foreheads. The sixth trumpet released angels of vengeance to destroy a third of the human race. An angel appeared, holding a scroll of prophecy, which John was told to eat, and false prophets were released to mislead humankind. At the sound of the seventh trumpet (chapter 11), accompanied by flashes of lightning and peals of thunder, God's sanctuary in heaven opened.

4 Apoc. 6:8

5 Apoc. 8:5

6 Apoc. 9:1

7 Apoc. 12:1

8 Apoc. 14:17

THE WOMAN CLOTHED WITH THE SUN

Now a dramatic vision follows (chapters 12 and 13) of a woman clothed with the sun and standing on the moon, understood in the medieval period as an allegory of the Church. Redon, who again eschewed a theological approach to the Apocalypse, depicted the woman with arms circled languorously above her head against a globe of light (number 7).

She gave birth and the child was pursued by a dragon, Satan, whom the Archangel Michael had cast out of heaven. Unable to catch the woman, the dragon pursued the rest of God's children, delegating the attack to a beast with seven heads and ten horns. The scene now returns to heaven (chapter 14), where the Lamb was seen standing on Mount Zion surrounded by the redeemed. Angels proclaimed reward for the just and punishment for the wicked. One angel urged a man sitting on a white cloud and holding a sickle to reap the harvest of the earth while another gathered the grapes that were put into the winepress of God's anger and crushed until blood flowed out. Redon depicts the reaper with an enormous sickle (number 8).

THE SEVEN PLAGUES AND THE WHORE OF BABYLON

Chapters 15 and 16 recount the final seven plagues from heaven: an affliction of disgusting sores struck mankind, the sea turned to blood, the rivers and springs turned to blood, the sun's heat began to burn humankind, darkness fell over earth, the kings of the East prepared for war at Armageddon, and destruction of the cities of the world commenced. Finally, Babylon, the Great Whore, was destroyed and the people of the world lamented for her (chapters 17 and 18).

THE MILLENNIUM

A huge crowd in heaven began to sing of victory, announcing the beginning of God's reign and the marriage feast of the Lamb (chapter 19). Now the last battle began, led by the warrior for justice mounted on a white horse. He defeated the seven-headed beast and threw him into a lake fiery with burning sulphur. An angel overpowered Satan, chained him up for a thousand years, and locked him in the abyss (Chapter 20). Redon shows us this angel, a figure of light, guiding a long chain downward (number 9) and also Satan, as a large snake coiled in darkness, enchained (number 10).

It is in the rather short chapter 20 that the millennium is described. During the "reign of a thousand years" some are raised from the dead and reign with Christ. Redon devotes two of his prints to chapter 20 (numbers 9 and 10), but focuses on the defeat of evil rather than the triumph of good. As suggested above, for many medieval exegetes the millennium corresponded to the historical moment in which they lived and referred, positively, to the triumph of the Church on earth. Historically, then, all of the dramatic events recounted in the first nineteen chapters of the Apocalypse had already occurred and the Heavenly Kingdom had defeated evil. Allegorically, however, the meaning of the events stood outside of time: God had punished, was now punishing, and would punish evildoers.

Returning to the sequence of events in the Apocalypse, at the end of this millennial reign of Christ Satan would be released for a short time and cause war all over earth until God consumed these forces of evil with fire and consigned them for eternity to the lake of sulphur. Redon shows Satan as a rather beautiful and sorrowful man, not a monster, emphasizing the devil's origin as the angel Lucifer, who fell from heaven because of his sin of pride (number 11).

9 Apoc. 20:1

10 Apoc. 20:2

11 Apoc. 20:10

THE HEAVENLY JERUSALEM

It is at the end of the millennium that the Last Judgment will take place and the dead will be raised and judged; those whose names are not found in the Book of Life are to be thrown into the fiery lake. But this judgment takes place neither on earth nor in heaven, for the original creation has ended and, along with it, time. Instead, John's vision is of the descent of the Heavenly Jerusalem, a new creation, which Redon imagines as a distant, light-filled city (number 12).

Only the last two chapters of the Apocalypse describe the Heavenly Jerusalem, the idea of which has so permeated the western European imagination, nourishing not only utopic writing and spirituality but also urban planning and architectural design. Above all, the Heavenly Jerusalem is a model of happiness and the plenitude of being: "Here God lives among men...He will wipe away all the tears from their eyes; there will be no more death, and no more mourning or sadness" (Apoc. 21:3–4). The river of life runs through it, flowing crystal clear, and its inhabitants will see God face to face in endless light and joy.

Redon closed his cycle with a portrait of John bearing his testimony (number 13): "I, John, am the one who heard and saw these things" (John 22:8). Perhaps we may understand this image metaphorically as a portrait of the artist, who once said that he never translated ideas from one medium (such as literature) to another (here, pictorial art) but only transcribed what he saw internally. In this sense, John's vision is Redon's own as well.

Throughout the *Apocalypse* series, Redon shows no interest in theology, allegory, or scriptural exegesis. Thus his interpretation differs from that of the Middle Ages in his choices of subjects to illustrate, in the literalism of his depictions, and in the personal rather than corporate emphasis of his images. And although his work was published in 1899, at the turn of the century, his series betrays no special concern with temporal thresholds. Yet insofar as Redon's series, depending on inner vision, provides a poetic and allusive rather than expository and analytical account of the Apocalypse it is consonant with the approach of the tenth and eleventh centuries, which stand at the center of our exhibition.

12 Apoc. 21:2

13 Apoc. 22:8

THE *MAIESTAS DOMINI*

The text of the Apocalypse ends with Jesus' promise about time: "I shall indeed be with you soon." The Second Coming of Christ can be thought of as an event in time, heralding the end of time at the end of the millennium. But it can also be understood as the full disclosure of a timeless reality. A reading on both the literal and spiritual levels is fostered by the similarity between John's two visions of the enthroned deity (the *Maiestas Domini*), one offered near the beginning and the other near the end of his book. Chapter 4 of the Apocalypse opens with a vision in which John was brought up to heaven and saw an enthroned person surrounded by twenty-four elders. The throne, circled by a rainbow, was attended by a lion, an eagle, a bull, and a man who, with the elders, worshiped the enthroned figure with song. This vision closely parallels the image that opens chapter 19 of the Apocalypse announcing the Last Judgment and both are indebted to Ezekiel's and Daniel's visions in the Old Testament (Ezek. 1:4–28; Dan. 10:5–6). However, while it is clearly God the Father who is enthroned in chapter 4, God the Son is enthroned as judge in chapter 19.

Although neither of these passages from the Apocalypse was of special interest to Redon, the *Maiestas Domini* is not only a frequent artistic subject in the medieval period but also almost the first, and by far the most common, subject chosen for the sculptural program of the main entrance of Romanesque churches. Its first appearance in that context, on the lintel of St.-Genis-des-Fontaines (France), occurred shortly after the year 1000. However, this iconographic subject appeared in art at least as early as the fifth and sixth centuries. One early example, a seventh-century ampulla in Bobbio (Italy), suggests a close relation between the subject and Holy Land pilgrimage. But others, such as that depicted in the façade mosaic of St. Peter's church in Rome (perhaps as early as the fifth century), may be more generally associated with the theology of the advent of the Heavenly Kingdom at the end of time. The *Maiestas Domini* is represented here by two works at radically different scale, which also suggest the diverse inflections of meaning that the general theme embraces. These works are a capital from Santa Maria de Lebanza (1185–1190, number 14) and Kenneth J. Conant's reconstruction of the lost tympanum (the space between the door lintel and the relieving arch above) from the third abbey church at Cluny in France (ca. 1115, number 15). While the capital is a relatively small work, originally placed above eye level and presumably one of a number of historiated capitals in the church interior, the lost tympanum was enormous and stood over the west portal as the main message for the spectator entering the church. Similar images, then, had entirely different placements and hermeneutic functions in our two examples.

The capital represents Christ enthroned and surrounded by the four beasts. Christ's hands are raised and his right side bared, displaying the wounds of the Crucifixion; four apostles (two on each of the lateral faces) carry instruments of the Passion. This iconography, closely associated with the Last Judgment, evokes chapter 19 of the Apocalypse and thus the end of the millennium. The capital may reflect the contemporaneous tympanum of the Portico de la Gloria at Santiago de Compostela in Spain, suggesting the miniaturization and transposition of a monumental composition.

14 Capital representing the *Maiestas Domini*

15 Tympanum of Cluny III representing the *Maiestas Domini*

According to Conant (to whom we will return in the next chapter), the *Maiestas Domini* portal at Cluny was as tall as a five- or six-story building (it measured forty-five feet in width and fifty-four feet in height), with the tympanum carved from a single stone weighing ten tons. The figure of Christ was twice life-size and, including the sculpture around the tympanum, about one hundred living beings were represented on the main portal. Although the portal was dynamited in the early nineteenth century, it is known from earlier engravings and from fragments recovered during excavation. As in number 14, the Christ figure was enthroned and surrounded by the four beasts. But instead of displaying the wounds of the crucifixion, his right hand was raised in blessing and he held a book (whether this was the scroll with seven seals or the Book of Life is not clear) in his left hand. His enthroned figure was carried in a mandorla (an aura of light) by angels standing on clouds.

Whether this monumental image was intended to evoke the Ascension (Acts 2:9–11); the Second Coming (chapter 4 of the Apocalypse, Luke 21:25-31, and the almost contemporary tympanum at Moissac in southern France); the Last Judgment (as in chapter 19 of the Apocalypse and the slightly later tympanum at the church of St.-Lazare at Autun in France); or was more generally a theophany (that is, a vision of the deity in his eternal reality) is not easy to determine. Although the tympanum displayed the composition most closely related to chapter 4 of the Apocalypse, representing God the Father, sculpture around and below the tympanum identify its subject as God the Son. Above the tympanum were two archivolts. The innermost contained fourteen angels; a fifteenth in the keystone held a sword and probably represented St. Michael. These, then, were the choirs of angels with Michael poised to destroy evil at the end of time. The outer archivolt had twenty-four heads—the twenty-four elders—and the keystone showed a head with a cross in its halo. The imagery of the archivolts, therefore, associated the tympanum with both chapters 4 and 19 of the Apocalypse. The lintel, however, had specifically christological associations. At far left and right were scenes of the Resurrection: the angel on the empty tomb addressing the three Marys (far left) and Mary Magdalene recognizing the risen Christ (far right). Its center was occupied by Mary, her hands upraised, flanked by the apostles. Read vertically together with the figure directly above, this scene can be understood as the Ascension of Christ. Temporally, then, the ensemble did not form a coherent narrative, combining instead narrative vignettes from the Resurrection and Ascension with God the Father or God the Son adored by angels and the twenty-four elders in heaven described in the Apocalypse.

One may conclude that the Cluny sculptor of the lost tympanum invested the traditional iconography of chapter 4 with the theological content of chapters 19 and 20 and that the portal's imagery was not primarily a logical exposition of theology any more than it was primarily a sequential narrative. The imagery is perhaps more fruitfully approached as a visualization of the eucharistic proclamation: "Christ has died, Christ is risen, Christ will come again." This liturgical prayer in turn recalls John's reference to Christ as the one "who is, who was, and who is to come" (Apoc. 1:4), repeated in the hymn that the animals sang around the throne: "Holy, Holy, Holy is the Lord, the Almighty; he was, he is, and he is to come" (Apoc. 4:8). From this hymn comes the text of the Sanctus sung at the Eucharist. But more generally, it epitomizes the central activity of Benedictine monasticism, which is the praise of God through the chanting of the Divine Office. Very likely, the meaning of the great tympanum at Cluny operated more profoundly on the spiritual and liturgical than on an historical level, embodying that paradoxical notion of the simultaneity of time and timelessness, so beautifully expressed by Paul when he referred to "the promised, expected, and at the same time already existing city [the Heavenly Jerusalem]" (Gal. 4:25–26), and inherent in the eucharistic liturgy.

This understanding of the intersection of the temporal and the eternal, the natural and the supernatural, had been perhaps most fully elaborated in Augustine's *City of God*, one of the most widely read books in the Middle Ages. And it is consonant with the spiritualized interpretation of the Apocalypse prevalent in the eleventh and early twelfth centuries. It is within this intellectual and spiritual context that Bernard of Clairvaux urged his monks to go on pilgrimage to Jerusalem not with their feet but by progressing with their inner being to the Heavenly Jerusalem. His metaphor of the spiritual life as pilgrimage, already fully developed by Augustine, is rooted in Paul's letter to the Hebrews, in which he recounts Abraham's journey to the Promised Land where "he looked forward to a city founded, designed and built by God" and says: "Here we do not have a lasting city; we seek a home that is yet to come" (Heb. 11:10 and 13:14). But this metaphor had explicit relevance for a period especially characterized by pilgrimage to holy sites—to Rome, Santiago de Compostela, and Jerusalem above all.

The "doctrine of the two cities" according to which the earthly Jerusalem is a type or figure of the Heavenly Jerusalem, inherent in Jesus' metaphorical language and made explicit by Paul, is the organizing concept of Augustine's *City of God*. It is also the underlying theme of this exhibition. Around the year 1000 this duality is frequently expressed in poetry, which more than prose is suited to its allusive and imaginative qualities. Cluniac culture especially was identified with the study and composition of poetry, and indeed was criticized on this account in the *Dialogue between a Cluniac and a Cistercian*, a tract written around 1135. Consider the following poetic evocation of the Heavenly Jerusalem, written by Bernard, a monk at Cluny at exactly this time:

> City of Zion, city fair, country of harmony and light. To thy joys art thou ever drawing the pious heart. Blessed Jerusalem, our home, not place of passage, street beautiful, Pythagoras' hand points the way to thy good gifts. Golden City of Zion, country of milk, beautiful in thy people, thou overwhelmest every heart, thou dazzlest the eye and heart of all. I cannot, cannot tell thy happiness and light, thy glad companionships, and thy wonderful glory. Trying to extol them, my heart is overcome and faints.

Bernard emphasizes emotion, especially desire and pleasure, as manifestations of hope, faith, and love: that is, of the theological virtues.

16 Capital representing the city of Emmaus

The journey toward recognition and vision was also expressed, metaphorically, by the biblical story of the Journey to Emmaus (Luke 24:13–35), in which the apostles walked and talked with the risen Christ without recognizing him until at supper, when their eyes were opened. A capital from St.-Pons-de-Thomières (ca. 1140, number 16) shows pilgrims with staffs walking on one side and the scene of recognition at the breaking of the bread on the other: the city of Emmaus is shown on one of the sides. Two tall, crenelated towers flank a lower central section in which there is an entrance. This is at once a representation of a city gate, following classical models, and an evocation of contemporaneous tripartite church façades (see number 20). Another capital at the Fogg Art Museum from Moûtiers-St.-Jean (ca. 1120, FAM 1922.17) depicts the same subject, but here the relation between the city of Emmaus and a church is explicit if, as has been suggested, it imitates forms from the surviving tower at Cluny. Emmaus, the city where the risen Christ was made known in the breaking of the bread, is the spiritual type of the church in which the eucharistic meal is celebrated. And the Eucharist, in turn, mystically enacts the marriage feast of the Lamb at the end of time, in the Heavenly Jerusalem.

Bibliographic Note

On time and the millennium, see Alfred Crosby, *The Measure of Reality. Quantification and Western Society, 1250–1600*, New York, 1997; Steven Jay Gould, *Questioning the Millennium*, New York, 1997; Anne Higgins, "Medieval Notions of the Structure of Time," *Journal of Medieval and Renaissance Studies*, 17, 1989, pp. 227–250; Germano Pàttaro, "The Christian Conception of Time," in *Cultures and Time*, eds. L. Gardet et al., Paris, 1976, pp. 169–195.

On the Apocalypse, see Yves Christe, *L'Apocalypse de Jean: Sens et développements de ses visions synthetiques*, Paris, 1996; and Peter K. Klein, *L'Apocalypse de Jean. Traditions exégétiques et iconographiques (III – XIIIe siècles*, Geneva, 1979. Beatus' Commentary is published as *Beati in Apocalipsin. Libri Duodecim*, ed. Henry Sanders, Rome, 1930. On the representation of the Apocalypse in art, the classic study is Frederik Van der Meer, *L'Apocalypse dans l'art*, Anvers, 1978. See more recently, Jerzy Miziolek, "When our Sun is Risen: Observations on Eschatological Visions in the Art of the First Millennium," *Arte Cristiana*, 83, 1995, pp. 3–22.

For Odilon Redon, see *Odilon Redon/Gustave Moreau/Rodolphe Bresdin*, ed. John Rewald, New York, 1962 (from which the quotations are taken); and for the *Apocalypse* series, André Mellerio, *L'Oeuvre graphique d'Odilon Redon*, Paris, 1913.

On the Cluny portal and the theme of the *Maiestas Domini* in Romanesque sculpture, see Kenneth J. Conant, "The Theophany in the History of Church Portal Design," *Gesta*, 15, 1976, pp. 127–134; Yves Christe, *Les Grands portails romans*, Geneva, 1969; and Calvin Kendall, *The Allegory of the Church. Romanesque Portals and Their Inscriptions*, Toronto, 1988.

On Cluniac spirituality, fundamental is Joan Evans, *Monastic Life at Cluny 910–1157*, London, 1931; Bernard of Cluny is quoted from Samuel Jackson, *The Source of "Jerusalem the Golden,"* Chicago, 1910, p. 111. Bernard of Clairvaux's instruction about pilgrimage is quoted from Ilene Forsyth's translation in "The *Vita Apostolica* and Romanesque Sculpture: Some Preliminary Observations," *Gesta*, 25, 1986, p. 79; and it is Forsyth who discusses the analogy with the Journey to Emmaus. The dialogue between the Cistercian and the Cluniac is discussed in Millard Hearn, *Romanesque Sculpture*, Ithaca, 1981, p. 116, n. 132.

The suggestion that the Moûtiers-St.-Jean capital imitates Cluny is in Walter Cahn and Linda Seidel, *Romanesque Sculpture in American Collections. Vol. I, New England Museums*, New York, 1979, p. 133; as is the proposed relation between the capital from Lebanza and the tympanum of the Portico de la Gloria at Santiago de Compostela.

17 Henry Hobson Richardson

the human architect and architecture made by human hands

CHRISTINE SMITH

The title *Before and After the End of Time: Architecture and the Year 1000* alludes to a dramatic contrast between architecture in western Europe from the seventh to tenth centuries on the one hand, and in the eleventh and twelfth centuries on the other. Whereas the earlier period saw very little building activity, and virtually no monumental architecture in quarried stone, the centuries after the turn of the millennium witnessed extensive construction of large-scale buildings accompanied by the revival of technology for building in stone. We are not suggesting a cause-and-effect relation between the failure of the world to end in 1000 and a renewed enthusiasm for the work of human hands. Nor is it the case that large stone buildings, which almost by definition require a knowledge of applied engineering and elaborate machines for the lifting and moving of weights, as well as abundant manpower and a great deal of money, appeared immediately after the turn of the millennium. Nonetheless, since a great many such buildings were begun in the eleventh century, whereas almost none had been attempted in the previous centuries, a general comparison between architecture before and after the year 1000 is appropriate.

ROMANESQUE ARCHITECTURE AND EARLY STUDY OF THE MEDIEVAL PERIOD

This change in the course of architecture is represented in the exhibition in various media, each illuminating a different aspect of the subject. We include photographs of existing buildings, twelfth-century sculpted depictions of architecture, elements of architectural sculpture from medieval buildings, and modern reconstructions of buildings before and after the millennium. Altogether these objects help viewers to understand the appearance, materiality, and conceptual organization of the new architecture. Additionally, however, because all these works are drawn from collections at Harvard University, a second theme emerges: the study of this material at the University. Just as in the preceding chapter the narrative of the Apocalypse was interwoven with an exposition of Redon's lithographs, so in this one the characteristics of architecture before and after the millennium will be intertwined with the story of how this material, neglected, obscured by later building campaigns (themselves the fruit of an increasing momentum in cut-stone engineering), and even destroyed between the sixteenth and nineteenth centuries, became first an object of visual interest, then of systematic scholarly study, and finally of graphic reconstruction based on archeological excavation. We trace this story through the paradigmatic contributions of three Harvard men: Henry Hobson Richardson, a Harvard graduate who became one of the foremost architects of the nineteenth century (number 17); Arthur Kingsley Porter, professor at Harvard in the early part of the twentieth century (number 41); and Kenneth J. Conant, trained as an architect at Harvard and later Porter's successor as professor of art history (number 42).

Photographs from Richardson's personal collection depicting San Michele in Pavia, San Zeno in Verona, the Abbaye des Dames in Caen, St. Gereon in Cologne, and the Cathedral in Trier (numbers 18, 19, 20, 21, and 22) attest to the first stirrings of modern interest in the Romanesque style, so central to Richardson's own architectural designs, and serve here to illustrate the general characteristics of the new architecture. Buildings during this period revived kinds of construction well established in classical antiquity such as stone masonry, vaulting, and the use of the Classical Orders. Even the use of figural sculpture as a means of expressing the "message" of the building, at first glance so medieval in approach, revives the practice of ancient Rome. It is because of this strongly classicizing tendency that architecture of the eleventh and early twelfth centuries is called Romanesque, meaning "Roman-like." By the mid-twelfth century, at least in the northwest of France, this classicizing style was supplanted by the first post-classical architectural style in Europe, the Gothic. Our exhibition, however, is concerned only with the Romanesque.

Although Romanesque buildings owe much to classical precedent, they also display entirely new features. Their innovations are by no means superficial but rather express the radically different mentality that had been born from the ruins of the classical world. Buildings, for instance, were now conceived in plan as comprised of modules, sometimes based on the square of the crossing (the juncture of nave and transepts) and sometimes on the square of the bay (defined at its corners by the nave columns or piers). The arithmetical proportions of the plan were expressed in elevation by the solid geometry of cylinders, cubes, and other regular solids, usually characterizing the exterior massing of the structure (see numbers 21 and 22). A supreme neatness, precision, and purity often informs the composition as a whole. Interior supports were often compound piers (masonry masses composed of columnar or quadrangular elements attached to a central core) rather than columns (see number 18). These great masses better withstood the weight and thrust of vaults, often themselves of stone. Visual relationships between the pier and vault were often expressed by wall responds—slender vertical elements attached to the wall (number 18). Much attention was paid to the mural boundary, which tended to be pierced with openings or developed sculpturally by groupings of shafts or moldings (see number 19). The contrast between the solidity and hardness of the building structure, its surfaces which catch light, and the piercing of that structure with openings in which shadows pool is evident in the photographs of San Zeno and the Abbaye des Dames (numbers 19 and 20). These qualities are further exemplified in the exhibition by the twelfth-century frieze and capital (numbers 23 and 24), both perhaps from Cluny. Miniature depictions of architecture, these reliefs nonetheless embody some of the aesthetic preferences of their monumental counterparts.

Often, Romanesque buildings articulate the great mass of the structure by including figures who "hold it up." While the interest in visually expressing weight and support relationships goes back to antiquity, as does the invention of caryatid figures, these acquire totally new and unexpected appearances on Romanesque buildings. We include two twelfth-century corbels, perhaps originally supporting the lintel of a doorway as we have exhibited them, or perhaps beneath a roofline, probably carved in the same geographic region as Cluny (numbers 25 and 26). They represent human caryatids who are not, like the main protagonists above the

18 San Michele in Pavia

19 San Zeno in Verona

20 Abbaye des Dames in Caen

23 Fragment of a frieze depicting architecture

24 Fragment of a capital depicting architecture

portal, messengers of Christian belief but rather are marginal, uncouth figures at liberty to exhibit and touch their most private parts. These sorts of obscene figures are not at all rare and their role in the overall iconographic program of Romanesque buildings is exceptionally difficult to determine. A quite frightening human face, probably a twelfth-century corbel or metope from western France, is another object of the same general type (number 27).

An especially clear example of the Romanesque interest in tectonic structure is the scene of Samson destroying the House of the Philistines on a twelfth-century capital from southern France (Judg. 16:23–31, number 28). If the fragile equipoise between the arch and its supports constitutes the main drama of this scene, the opposite side shows the enormous strength of Samson in his ability to carry off the gates of Gaza on his shoulders (Judg. 16:1–3). The illustration of this biblical narrative, then, assumes a spectator who recognizes the essential constructional principle of load and support. While the Samson capital played on that knowledge for dramatic purposes, the columnar support from Santiago de Compostela, where three apostles are attached to or rather are themselves a column, exploits that understanding to visualize a metaphor (number 29). Presumably one of four such pedestals, the twelve apostles "supported" some kind of liturgical furniture, probably an altar. Translating this visual metaphor into words, one could say that the liturgy of the Church has an apostolic basis. Almost all Romanesque sculpture is an integral part of a building and is placed where the structure offers opportunity: in the tympanum (number 15); as a capital above a column or pilaster (numbers 14, 30, and 31); as an abacus between the capital and an arch (number 32); supporting the roof (number 33); or in the spandrels between arches (numbers 34 and 35). Romanesque sculpture is so closely integrated with its architectural setting that buildings can often be dated and their stylistic qualities exemplified through analysis of capitals, friezes, profiles, and other carved work. Most of the ambitious new projects begun in the eleventh century took decades to construct, and this is one reason why the majority of our sculptural examples are of the twelfth rather than of the eleventh century.

The key importance of architectural sculpture was intuited by Arthur Kingsley Porter, who created a systematic photographic archive of such material: we include five of his photos in our exhibition (numbers 36, 37, 38, 39, and 40). Professor at Harvard from 1920 to 1933, Kingsley Porter's work on *The Construction of Lombard and Gothic Vaults* appeared in 1911 and his multi-volume *Lombard Architecture* in 1915. The evolution of scholarly interest in the Romanesque since Richardson is suggested by a portrait of Kingsley Porter posed with his wife Lucy before a Lombard Romanesque church (number 41). He is shown in a motor car, evidently and appropriately en route, since his most influential publication was *Romanesque Sculpture of the Pilgrimage Roads* (1928). Study, in other words, had moved from a focus on isolated monuments to the hypothesizing of broad groups of works related geographically, by the diffusion of artistic ideas due to phenomena such as pilgrimage, or by shared formal qualities constituting a "school." Kingsley Porter contributed greatly to the acquisition of Romanesque sculpture by the Fogg Art Museum, valuing the works not only for their aesthetic qualities but also as historical evidence. Four of the pieces in our exhibition were acquired by the museum during his tenure (numbers 14, 16, 28, and 29). The magnificent capitals from Moûtiers-St. Jean in the portico of the Fogg Museum courtyard were also acquired at this time

25 and 26 Corbels representing crouching human figures

27 Corbel or metope representing a human face

28 Capital representing Samson destroying the House of the Philistines

29 Columnar support with the apostles Matthias, Jude, and Simon

30 Capital with acanthus leaves

31 Fragment of a capital

32 Abacus with rinceau of leaves and beaded interlace

33 Corbel representing a cow

34 Spandrel with a saint, hind, and hunter

35 Spandrel with a wreath of leaves enclosing pinecones

36 Tomb of Abbot Isarne (d. 1048) at St.-Victoire in Marseilles

37 Gospel Book, Vich, Episcopal Museum (mss. 89)

38 Capital with apostles and symbol of St. Luke

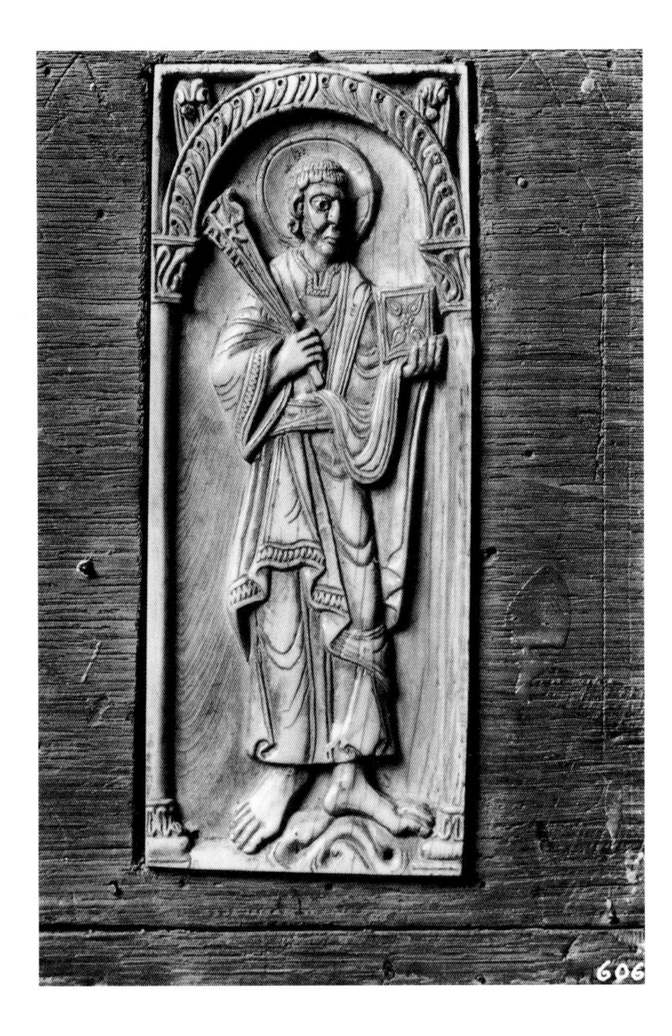

39 Reliquary of St. John the Baptist, detail of St. Peter

40 South cross, east face, at Castledermot in County Kildare

41 Arthur Kingsley Porter and Lucy Porter in their car

(FAM 1922.16–27; 1922.7;1925.9.1). The very fine piece from Santiago de Compostela (number 29), goal of the pilgrimage route most closely studied by Kingsley Porter, installed at the entrance to our exhibition was a gift to Harvard from the Republic of Spain negotiated by the scholar (as was also FAM 1933.99 a and b): he published it in his *Spanish Romanesque Sculpture* in 1928. Some of Kingsley Porter's students became important collectors of Romanesque sculpture—John Nicholas Brown, for instance (Harvard, Class of 1922)—and his connections with other Harvard graduates who collected facilitated both loans and exhibitions. One such was John Pierpont Morgan (Class of 1889), whose manuscript of Beatus' *Commentary on the Apocalypse* has served as our template image for the Heavenly Jerusalem. Kingsley Porter's widow Lucy left another three Romanesque sculptures to the Fogg at her death. (FAM 1962.317, 1962.320, and 1962.321). Vézelay was an important goal of pilgrimage since the church of La Madeleine possessed relics of Mary Magdalene; Conant would later suggest that it was on a main route to Santiago. The exhibition includes two twelfth-century spandrels, perhaps from the cloister at Vézelay (number 34 and 35). One of these is historiated and shows a scene that has been identified as St. Giles (or Gilles) protecting a hind from a hunter's arrow. Since Giles was a medieval saint especially revered in Arles, this suggests the interregional character of Romanesque art and the importance of the pilgrimage routes in the diffusion of culture. An eleventh-century Spanish reliquary that Kingsley Porter photographed also makes this point. One of its sides depicts St. Peter (number 39), whose tomb was the principal focus of pilgrimage to Rome, while another side shows St. Michael the Archangel, whose veneration was expressed in pilgrimage to sites stretching from Mont-St.-Michel in Normandy to Monte Sant'Angelo in southeast Italy.

KENNETH J. CONANT

AND THE ABBEY OF CLUNY

The portrait of Kenneth J. Conant (1894–1984) seated in the excavation site at Cluny in 1931 reflects a subsequent phase in Romanesque scholarship (number 42). The excavations were begun under Kingsley Porter with the sponsorship of the Medieval Academy of America in 1927–1928, but Conant was the leader of this project almost from its inception until 1950. Some of Conant's original drawings, many of which are preserved at Harvard's Graduate School of Design, are included in the exhibition. Although Kingsley Porter had been the first to recognize the hand of the so-called "Cluny Master" at both Cluny III and Vézelay, Conant would make the reconstruction of Cluny in all its phases his central intellectual and artistic project. Indeed, it was Conant who identified as St. Peter the half-length male figure acquired in 1920 by the museum of the Rhode Island School of Design, which came from the west portal of Cluny III and is considered to be the most significant fragment from the monastery in existence outside of France.

Cluny, a reformed Benedictine monastery in Burgundy founded in A.D. 909/910, was almost entirely demolished during and after the French Revolution (1798–1823) when all monasteries were suppressed and the possessions of the French Church confiscated. Two sculptures from or near Cluny itself (numbers 23 and 24) and other examples from closely related structures in the vicinity (numbers 25, 26, 30, 34, and 35) all give an idea of its distinctive sculptural style, formative for Burgundian Romanesque architectural sculpture.

42 Kenneth J. Conant in an excavation trench at Cluny, 1931

No better example could be chosen to exemplify the course of medieval architecture around the year 1000 than the successive building campaigns at Cluny. This monastery church so flourished in our period that it was enlarged twice in two hundred years; these successive structures are referred to as Cluny I, II, and III. Cluny II, built between 955 and 981, was one of the largest buildings in western Europe with a length of over 150 feet. The addition of vaulting between 1002 and 1018 made it one of the first large-scale vaulted structures to have been erected in the West since antiquity. Cluny II alone would have made an interesting paradigm of the course of western European architecture before and after the millennium. We show Conant's reconstruction of the church and abbey as seen from the west (number 43). Yet Cluny II was as nothing compared to Cluny III, begun in 1088 and consecrated in 1130 (number 44). The nave of Cluny III was 425 feet long, 40 feet wide, and 100 feet high (number 45). The revival of monumental stone architecture after 1000 progressed so rapidly that an outstanding building at the turn of the millennium was quickly replaced by one so large, so skillfully conceived, and so richly ornamented that it was hardly rivaled up to the time of its destruction.

An early manifestation of Conant's enthusiasm for Cluny, and one of his many ingenious ideas for making this medieval marvel real for an American public, was the erection of a plaster, wood, and beaverboard replica of the choir of Cluny in the courtyard of the Fogg Art Museum in 1932–1933. Although this immense structure, forty-five-feet tall, filled the courtyard as we see in a contemporary photograph (number 46), it was only one-half the height of the original apse at Cluny. Conant had been trained as an architect (indeed, his master's thesis was a project for a monastery in Cambridge) and his design skills are evident in his graphic representations of the various phases of development of this Burgundian monastery. His drawing of the plan of the apse is based on his firsthand knowledge of the excavation: he includes measurements as well as the dedications of the chapels and altars (number 47). Conant's reconstructions are, perforce, hypothetical, since so little remains of the original complex, and they betray by their completeness and realism his desire to bring the past to life through visualization. Especially striking is the brightly colored drawing of the east end of Cluny III with its extraordinary exterior massing of chapels, apse, transept, and towers to which Conant appended a partial plan of the same area (number 44). A collage in which Conant drew around a photo of one of the Cluny capitals (number 48) in order to supply a sense of its architectural context and another collage in which the abbey is superimposed on a photo of the modern town of Cluny (number 49) are other such devices.

This concern with context also reveals Conant's intuition that the monastery church of Cluny was not the sole object of research but rather was the culminating feature of an entire complex of buildings. These included dormitories, refectory, meeting hall, library, infirmary, guest accommodations, workshops, stables, baths, cloisters, and gardens, as well as a cemetery (number 43). Altogether—and this is what Conant's general views of the entire complex suggest—the Cluny complex embodied a way of life based on clearly defined values. As such it was the visible manifestation of its citizens' way of life; in short, a city. Cluny's abbots were fully aware of the relation between the monastery and the heavenly city. Abbot Odon (927–942) viewed the church in which the monks sang the Divine Office as "their Jerusalem having descended from the heavens," the goal toward which Bernard of Cluny's poem (quoted in the previous essay) so ardently longs, and Abbot Peter the Venerable (1122–1156) described Cluny III as a celestial citadel constantly besieged by the Devil, who was jealous of its virtue. We will return to the relation between the church made by human hands and the Heavenly Jerusalem in our next chapter.

43 Cluny II from the west

44 View of Cluny III from the east, with partial plan attached

45 Perspective view of the interior of Cluny III

46 Kenneth J. Conant with his installation of the apse of Cluny in the Fogg Art Museum courtyard, 1934

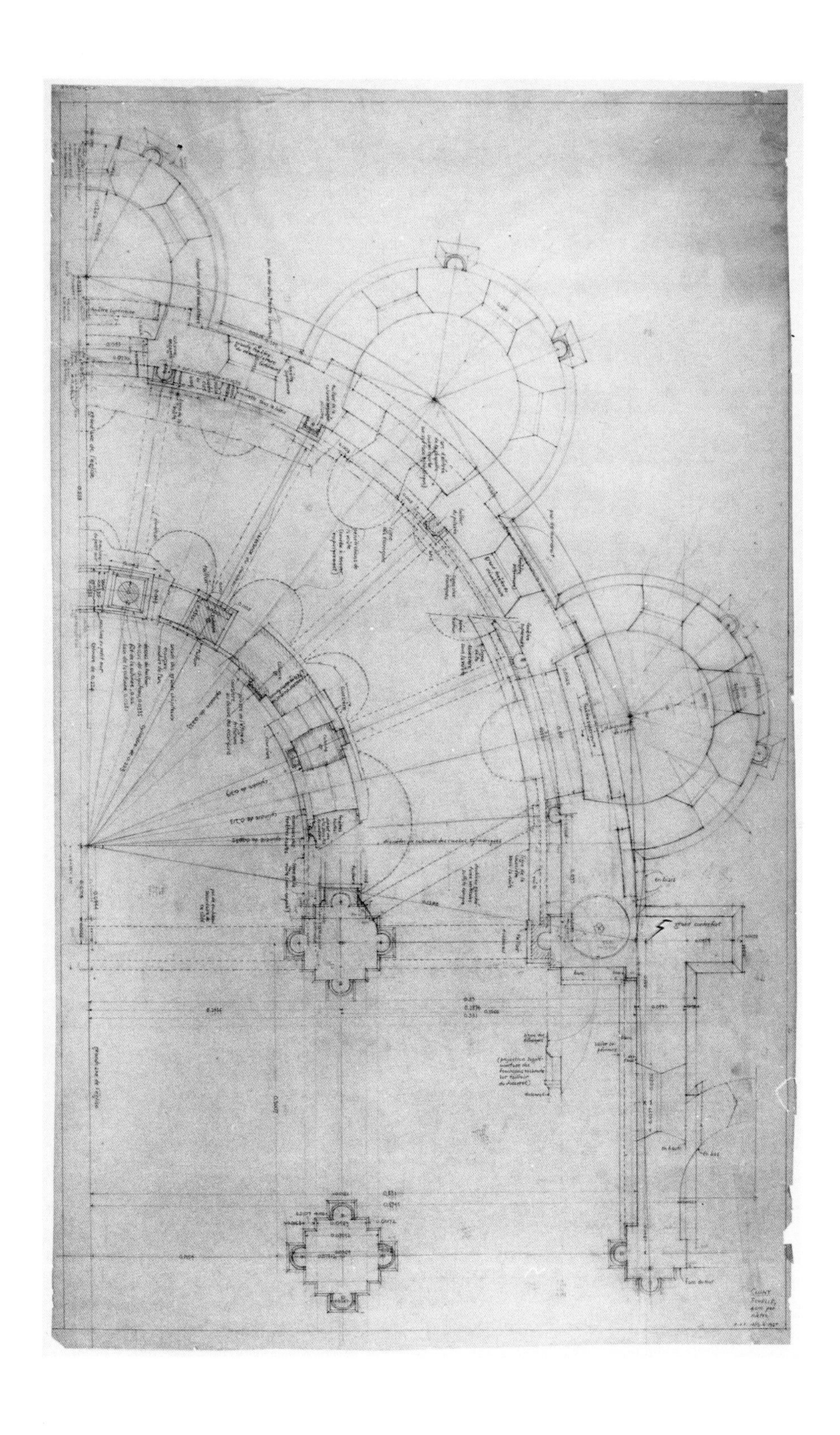

47 Plan, apse of Cluny III

THE ARCHITECT

The new buildings of the eleventh and twelfth centuries were the fruit of human labor, the work of human hands. What happened to the human artificer before and after the year 1000 to so alter his aims and his means? The status of the architect in regard to his professional knowledge (as distinct from, for instance, his social status) was low in the centuries before the millennium. Western Europe inherited from classical antiquity a disdain for manual as opposed to intellectual labor. However, most classical thinkers, including Plato and Aristotle, considered the crafts to be of a higher order than were merely physical tasks because they were based on rational and orderly method, and on principles that could be taught. Moreover, the crafts introduced order into disorder and involved skillful action directed toward a clearly conceived and good end. Hence architecture could be considered an "art" and not just a knack, inspiration, or physical exertion. For the Romans, the mechanical art (*ars mechanica*) meant the art of making war engines, astronomical models, and lifting devices, and Vitruvius included these and other activities in his first-century-B.C. treatise on architecture.

However, in the wake of a general cultural and economic decline from the fifth to seventh century, the actual practice of architecture declined and its status, already not elevated, sank. Yet its earlier status was retained, exceptionally, by Isidore of Seville (ca. 570–636) who claimed mechanics to be one of the seven branches of physics along with arithmetic, geometry, music, astronomy, astrology, and medicine, and hence a branch of philosophy. Whether or not Isidore was simply repeating a categorization from some earlier author, his inclusion opened the possibility, not fully explored until the twelfth century, that mechanics involved both theoretical knowledge and manual labor or, at the least, an abstract principle behind the fabrication of things. Isidore was widely read in the Middle Ages (the texts inscribed on the Morgan Beatus are quotations from him), as was Rhabanus Maurus (780–856), who repeated Isidore's inclusion of mechanics as a part of physics. But although the art of mechanics overlapped with that of building, it was by no means coterminous with it. Isidore's discussion of architecture does not suggest that building involves theoretical knowledge of any kind. The builder is not an architect (the word "architect" means "chief artificer") but a manual laborer identified with the material that he manipulates: *caementarius* (mason), *lathomus* (stoneworker), or *carpentarius* (carpenter).

The term "mechanical arts," used as a parallel to, but also in counterdistinction from, "liberal arts" first appeared in John Scottus Eriugena's ninth-century commentary on Martianus Capella's *The Marriage of Philology and Mercury*. The liberal arts, Eriugena said, were inherent in human understanding and are therefore natural, whereas the mechanical arts were first invented by humankind. While this might seem a positive definition for the latter, Eriugena continued that the liberal arts, which have their source and goal in the soul, serve the soul, whereas the mechanical arts, whose source and goal is outside the soul, serve the body. Undoubtedly, architecture serves the human physical need for shelter, involves manual labor, and is done for pay. Thus in antiquity it was appropriate work for persons of low status and on the same level as weaving, agriculture, or navigation. However, medieval attitudes toward manual labor and class were ambivalent: Jesus himself had been a carpenter, Paul a tentmaker, and Peter a fisherman. Further, it could be supposed that Adam and Eve were occupied with manual labor in the Garden of Eden even before the Fall. Moreover, St. Benedict's monastic Rule, which dominated western monasticism until the twelfth century, explicitly required monks to alternate manual

48 Capital from Cluny III

49 Cluny superimposed on the town of Cluny

labor with intellectual and spiritual labor. Indeed, central to the foundation of the Cistercian Order (1109) was the reaffirmation of this requirement, which had been neglected in monasteries of the Cluniac obedience. A more positive attitude toward human labor, in relation to an increased concern with time and how people use it, is evident in depictions in calendars and church portals of the labors of the months, popular in the twelfth century. At least by this century, the participation of laymen in the manual work of constructing churches was considered a pious act. The theology of labor, then, could theorize work as a punishment resulting from Adam's Fall or as a God-given grace by means of which human beings could participate in God's plan for salvation. This second view, for instance, was advocated by Rupert of Deutz (ca. 1070–1129/30) when he explained that "skilled craftsmen ought to be admonished lest they devote divine skill to the pursuit of gain, for their talents are not their own, but bestowed on them by their creator, and that which he has given he will also require."

As in so many other areas, the eleventh century presents an enigma in regard to the image of the architect. Although architecture was classed as a mechanical art whose practitioners were termed according to the physical material that they worked, an exceptionally large number of patrons, many aristocratic and all wealthy and educated, seem to have acted as architects, not only designing buildings but also overseeing their construction. Bishop Bernward of Hildesheim and Abbot Desiderius of Montecassino are but the most famous of these. The tombstone of Abbot Isarne (number 36) shows us a portrait of a man of this class, although we do not know the degree of his involvement in the building of St.-Victoire at Marseilles, completed some eight years before his death in 1048. Another large category of educated, upper-class people who were not themselves patrons also acted as architects. Bishop Benno of Osnabrück and Bishop Otto of Bamberg had such a role at Speyer Cathedral and Hézelon of Liège, a canon, seems to have designed and/or built Cluny III. It may be supposed that in some cases acting as an architect meant practical application of principles learned in the liberal arts, especially geometry, arithmetic, and harmonic theory (music), although in others it surely included actual physical work. How the educated elite learned the practice of architecture and precisely what its procedures were in the eleventh century has yet to be discovered.

For the twelfth century the evidence is more abundant. Especially important are the writings of Hugh of St. Victor (ca. 1096–1141), a German canon regular who spent most of his career in Paris. Hugh considered mechanics one of the four branches of philosophy because since one of the aims of philosophy was to remedy weakness in the body, the study of technology, which enables us to supply our physical wants, was essential to a philosophical education. While for Hugh the actual practice of the mechanical arts was unsuitable for upper-class people, Honorius of Autun (ca. 1080–1137) suggested that mechanics, along with medicine and economics, were actually liberal arts—that is, based on theoretical knowledge—and appropriate activities for the educated elite. The new, higher status of mechanics in the twelfth century was partly a response to the technological inventions and the rising European economy dependent on them as well as to an increasing belief in the moral goodness of technology and material progress. In architecture, the new technology made possible stone quarrying and transport, devices for carving stone blocks, and machinery for lifting them into place. Applied geometry made possible stereotomy (the art of cutting solids), the calculation of vault curvatures, and the elaboration of complex plan designs such as that of the apse of Cluny III (number 47).

Contemporaries seem to have been uncertain as to whether these achievements were due to human skill, divine intervention, or magic. In his very popular *History of the Kings of Britain* (1136), Geoffrey of Monmouth tells the story of how Aurelius, wanting to build a great memorial, assembled carpenters and stone masons and asked them to design something worthy. This they were unable to do. He then summoned the magician Merlin, who advised him to take the Giant's Ring from Mount Killaraus in Ireland. This Ring was made of enormous stones having medicinal properties, which Giants had brought from Africa. When Aurelius' masons were unable to move the stones with hawsers and ropes, Merlin, using a gear mechanism, lifted the stones, transported them by ship, and re-erected them at Salisbury, "thus proving that his artistry was worth more than any brute strength." However, in an analogous story of almost the same date recounted by Abbot Suger of St. Denis, in *De Consecratione,* a problem of lifting and transporting columns that had defeated the workers was resolved by some weak and disabled persons together with a few boys who, by the power of prayer, were able to move the mass that usually required more than a hundred strong men.

The wonder, and even incredulity, which feats of engineering elicited in the eleventh and twelfth centuries was associated with the discovery of something never before seen—that is, with invention. It is not surprising that the term *ingeniatores*—meaning "engineers"—first appeared in 1058, referring to men in charge of military machines, or that the only instance of a medieval artist being acclaimed for his *ingenium* is an inscription of 1106 praising the architect of Modena cathedral, Lanfranco. The Latin term is close to the English words "ingenious" and "ingenuity," referring to mental acuity but above all to clever invention or discovery.

It is this period of optimism and delight in the work of human hands that gave birth to the new architecture after the millennium. The sheer size and technical difficulty of the new buildings expressed the confidence of their makers in the power of the human mind and hands to make buildings that could be compared to the Heavenly Jerusalem. But only God, the supreme architect, creator of the world itself could build the Heavenly City at the end of time:

> Then the One sitting on the throne spoke:
> "Now I am making the whole of creation new"
> he said. (Apoc. 21:5)

Bibliographic Note

For Romanesque sculpture in the Fogg Art Museum, the best source is Walter Cahn and Linda Seidel, *Romanesque Sculpture in American Collections. Volume I. New England Museums*, New York, 1979, with bibliography. See also Seidel's "Romanesque Sculpture in American Collections. IX. The William Hayes Fogg Art Museum," *Gesta*, 11, 1972, pp. 59–80 and her "Romanesque Sculpture in American Collections. X. The Fogg Art Museum," *Gesta*, 12, 1973, pp. 57–81. For the history of the collection there is a recent study by Kathryn McClintock, "Academic Collecting at Harvard," in Elizabeth Smith, ed., *Medieval Art in America: Patterns of Collecting 1800–1940*, University Park, 1996, pp. 173–181.

On Cluny the fundamental work remains Kenneth Conant's *Cluny. Les églises et la maison du chef d'ordre*, Mâcon, 1968; the most recent overview is Dominique Vingtain, *L'Abbaye de Cluny. Centre de l'occident médiéval*, Paris, 1998. The bibliography of the excavations at Cluny can be found in Jacques Stiennon, "Hézelon de Liège, architecte de Cluny III," in *Mélanges offerts à René Crozet*, eds. P. Gallais and Y. Riou, Poitiers, 1966, vol. I, pp. 345–358; and Francis Salet, "Cluny III," *Bulletin Monumentale*, 126, 1968, pp. 235–292.

On the history of craft and the status of architecture, a very thorough survey is Elspeth Whitney, *Paradise Restored. The Mechanical Arts from Antiquity through the Thirteenth Century*, Transactions of the American Philosophical Society, 80, 1990. Also excellent is George Ovitt, *The Restoration of Perfection. Labor and Technology in Medieval Culture*, New Brunswick, 1987. In German, Peter Sternagel, *Die Artes Mechanicae im Mittelalter. Begriffs- und Bedeutungs-geschichte bis aum Ende des 13. Jahrhunderts*, Munich, 1966. See also Jacques Le Goff, *Time, Work, and Culture in the Middle Ages*, Chicago, 1980; and Jacqueline Hamesse and Colette Muraille-Samaran, eds., *Le Travail au môyen age: Une approache interdisciplinaire*, Louvain-la Neuve, 1990.

On the medieval architect, see Douglas Knoop and G. P. Jones, *The Medieval Mason*, Manchester, 1933; and more recently, Günther Binding, *Der Früh- und Hochmittelalterliche Bauherr als Sapiens Architectus*, Cologne, 1996; and Charles Radding and William Clark, *Medieval Architecture, Medieval Learning: Builders and Masters in the Age of Romanesque and Gothic*, New Haven, 1992. Many of the primary sources are gathered in Victor Mortet, *Recueil des textes relatifs à l'histoire de l'architecture*, Paris, 1911–1929. Also of interest are Carolyn Carty, "The Role of Gunzo's Dream in the Building of Cluny," *Gesta*, 27, 1988, pp. 113–123; Mary Carruthers, "The Poet as Master-Builder: Composition and Locational Memory in the Middle Ages," *New Literary History*, 24, 1993, pp. 881–904; and Merriam Sherwood, "Magic and Mechanics in Medieval Fiction," *Studies in Philology*, 44, 1947, pp. 567–592 (where the story about Merlin is recounted).

On building procedures and technology, some classic studies are Paul Frankl, "The Secret of the Mediaeval Masons," *Art Bulletin*, 27, 1945, pp. 46–64, and the series of articles on medieval construction by Marcel Aubert in *Bulletin monumental* in 1960 and 1961. There is abundant recent bibliography, such as John Fitchen, *Building Construction before Mechanization*, Cambridge (MA), 1986; Francis and Joseph Gies, *Cathedral, Forge and Waterwheel. Technology and Invention in the Middle Ages*, New York, 1994; Jean Gimpel, *The Medieval Machine: The Industrial Revolution of the Middle Ages*, Harmondsworth, 1976; Jacques Heyman, *The Stone Skeleton: Structural Engineering of Masonry Architecture*, New York, 1995.

Lynn White has studied the cultural implications of medieval technology in a number of publications, including "Cultural Climates and Technological Advance in the Middle Ages," *Viator*, 2, 1971, pp. 171–201; "The Iconography of 'Temperantia' and the Virtuousness of Technology," in *Action and Conviction*, eds. Rabb and Siegel, pp. 197–219; and "Medieval Engineering and the Sociology of Knowledge" in his *Medieval Religion and Technology. Collected Essays*, Berkeley, 1978, pp. 317–338. See also Ernst Benz, "The Christian Expectation of the End of Time and the Idea of Technical Progress," in his *Evolution and Christian Hope: Man's Concept of the Future from the Early Fathers to Teilhard de Chardin*, Garden City, 1966.

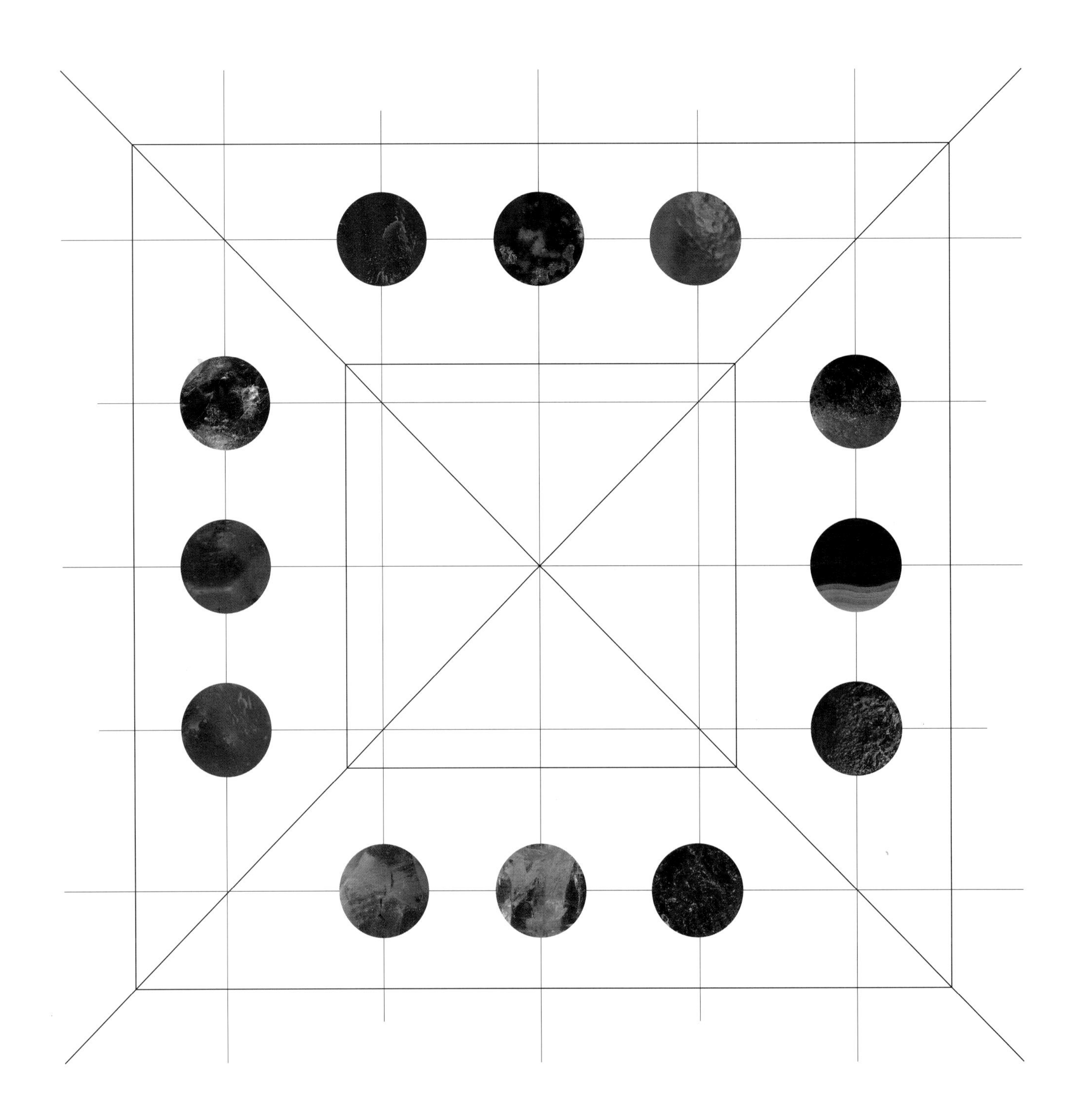

50 Geometric abstraction of the Morgan Beatus with gemstones

the divine architect and the heavenly jerusalem

CHRISTINE SMITH

Medieval Christianity held in common with Judaism the belief that God created all things, seen and unseen. As the early Church defined its place in relation to other systems of belief, especially pagan philosophy and cosmology, the manner of this creation was much discussed. Since Plato's account was quite close to Christian belief in many ways, a clear distinction was drawn between the Christian God's creative act *ex nihilo* (from nothing) and that of Plato's Demiurge, who introduced order into eternally existing matter. So central is the Christian understanding of God as creator that it is the subject of the twenty-four elders' praise in the *Maiestas Domini* of Apoc. 4:8: "You are our Lord and our God, you are worthy of glory and honor and power, because you made all the universe and it was only by your will that everything was made and exists."

The Christian distinction between creating and making also set God's activity apart from that of the human artisan who shapes things out of preexisting matter. The absolutely unique character of God's creativity is an unchanging tenet of medieval theology, reiterated from St. Augustine in the fifth century—"the creature cannot create" (*De Trinitate* 3:9)—to St. Thomas Aquinas in the thirteenth.

In addition to creating, God also makes things. Although in the accounts in Genesis the creation of the cosmos is a pure act of will expressed in words, elsewhere in Scripture the terminology of creation is that of building. Indeed, the verb "to build" and its derivatives appear 360 times in the Septuagint (the Greek translation of the Old Testament). Thus in Ecclesiasticus we read that: "The Lord has not granted to the holy ones to tell of all His marvels which the Almighty Lord has solidly constructed for the universe to stand firm in His glory" (42:17). In Isaiah, God is said to have measured the water of the sea in the hollow of his hand, calculated the dimensions of the heavens, and weighed the hills in a balance (40:12); he "stretched out the heavens like a cloth, spread them like a tent for men to live in" (40:22). Perhaps most influential was the eulogy, attributed to Solomon, of God's relation to his creation: "your all-powerful hand did not lack means/—the hand that from formless matter created the world—/... But no, you ordered all things by measure, number and weight" (Wisd. of Sol., 11:17–18 and 11:21). This implied that while God is able to create by fiat, God chooses to create in accordance with the natural law he established. Because of this a certain analogy between the human and divine artificer can be drawn and God's creation can be thought about in architectural terms. So St. Augustine asks: "But by what means did you make heaven and earth? What tool did you use for this vast work?" (*Confessions* 11:5).

Not only has God made things "with His hands," but he instructs human beings how to make things: Noah, the Ark (Gen. 6:13–16); Moses, the Tabernacle (Exod. 26). And God sanctified with his presence buildings made for him, most importantly, Solomon's Temple (1 Kings 5:15–6:38). After its destruction, God's angels showed prophets visions of the future temple (Ezek. 40–44, Tob. 13:9–23, and Dan. 40–43) and God himself ordered Haggai to prophesy the "new glory" of the rebuilt temple (Hag. 1:9). At the end of time, God will create a new heaven and a new earth, making all things new (Isa. 65:17). This is the Heavenly Jerusalem, the descent of which concludes John's vision in the Apocalypse. Early on, Christians interpreted prophecies of the new Temple as metaphors for the true temple, that is, the temple not built by human hands. This surely underlies Paul's statement that:

> We have no eyes for things that are visible, but only for things that are invisible; for visible things last only for a time, and the invisible things are eternal. For we know that when the tent that we live in on earth is folded up, there is a house built by God for us, an everlasting home not made by human hands, in the heavens." (2 Cor. 4:18–5:1)

St. Augustine, following Paul, interpreted Haggai's prophecy of the new temple as an architectural metaphor for this eternal home, which is the City of God (*City of God* 18.48). In this approach, Solomon's building became a prototype or prefigurement of the Heavenly Jerusalem, city of peace.

By the eighth century, biblical exegesis had become more formally structured. Thus the Venerable Bede, explaining the significance of the Church, said that literally, the Church was the Temple of Solomon; that typologically (allegorically), it was Christ or the Virgin; tropologically (ethically), the communion of the faithful; and anagogically (spiritually), the Heavenly Jerusalem (*De Schematibus et tropis*). Bede was less interested in architectural form than in architectural significance. Thus the place of union between God and humankind might variously be a single building, a person or group of people, or a city. Before exploring the implications of this kind of exegesis for architecture it will be useful to complete our discussion of God as architect.

The Christian idea of God as creator and maker tended, after the year 1000, to foster the image of the Divine Architect, depicted holding scales, a carpenter's square, and/or a pair of compasses or dividers. Such images—over forty exist in which God holds compasses—have been related to specific passages in the Old Testament such as: "When He fixed the heavens firm, I was there,/when He drew a ring on the surface of the deep" (Prov. 8:27). Their diffusion after 1000 has been associated variously with Rabbinical exegesis, the Platonism of the School of Chartres, the refutation of Cathar dualism, or St. Augustine's commentary on Genesis. Whatever its intellectual matrix, the image of the Divine Architect affirms the goodness of the created world, the analogy between human and divine making, and the importance of technology.

Theological consideration of God as an architect is, correspondingly, more prominent around 1100 than previously. Gerhoch of Reichersberg (1092–94 to 1169) devoted an entire work to the subject, the *Liber de aedificio Dei*, and William of Conches (ca. 1080–1154) compared the operation of the human and divine architect in his *Commentary on the Timaeus*. God, he said, creates *ex nihilo* without resistance of matter and without external pressure; the human architect transforms preexisting matter, which resists, acting on needs that he doesn't control. God's work is permanent, man's perishes; God's work is perfect and corresponds exactly to divine intention whereas human work is deficient. God's creation is an adequate expression of God's intelligence, whereas human beings are incapable of conceiving all they wish or realizing all they conceive. Alain de Lille (ca. 1125/30–1203), the last great spokesman of the School of Chartres, essentially repeated William's comparison in his *De Planctu naturae*, concluding that God was the elegant architect who made the universe as his palace.

The comparison between the divine and human builder further illuminates our capital with scenes from the life of Samson (number 28), since it assumes a spectator aware of human limitation and divine omnipotence. It is the resistance of matter, its measure and number and weight, which makes Samson's feats of carrying off the Gates of Gaza and destroying the House of the Philistines so astonishing. The sculptor emphasizes Samson's physical effort, showing his body curved and twisted as he struggles against nature. Yet God, by contrast, can make the entire heavens and earth pass away by the same pure act of intellect by which he created them, as John tells us.

The theology of God as an architect has a counterpart in the Pauline notion of humankind as God's fellow worker. "By the Grace God gave me," Paul says, "I succeeded as an architect and laid the foundations.... On this foundation you can build in gold, silver and jewels, or in wood, grass and straw, but whatever the material, the work of each builder is going to be clearly revealed when the day comes" (1 Cor. 3:10–15). Paul's metaphor refers to the edifice of faith, "built up" by Christians: "Didn't you realize that you were God's temple and that the Spirit of God was living among you? If anybody should destroy the temple of God, God will destroy him, because the temple of God is sacred; and you are that temple." The Last Judgment is the test of the builders' work, and Paul implies that the true temple is not a building in Jerusalem or even a new construct created by God as the Heavenly Jerusalem, but is constituted by individuals' faith. He sustains this metaphor in the Letter to the Ephesians: "You are part of a building that has the apostles and prophets for its foundations, and Jesus Christ himself for its main cornerstone. As every structure is aligned on him, all grow into one holy temple in the Lord; and you too, in him, are being built into a house where God lives, in the Spirit" (2:21–22). Paul's imagery is repeated in John's description of the Heavenly Jerusalem in the Apocalypse: "The city walls stood on twelve foundation stones, each one of which bore the name of one of the twelve apostles" (21:14). The columnar support from Santiago de Compostela (number 29) visualizes this metaphor but it is even more explicitly illustrated by the Heavenly Jerusalem from the Morgan Beatus manuscript, which serves as the template for our image of the Heavenly City in the exhibition (number 1). Here the apostles are placed in the gates of the city, following Augustine's claim that they are the doors through which we enter the Kingdom of God.

Given this strong tradition of metaphorical expression, it is not surprising that Beatus of Liébana's eighth-century commentary on the Apocalypse does not devote much space to architectural description. As he says, all of the description of the Heavenly Jerusalem in Apocalypse, chapter 21, is to be understood in the spiritual sense as referring to the saints, with whom God will dwell (12:5 and 8). This interpretation is consonant with the allegorical and moralizing approach of Beatus' commentary in general and is typical of the period. This is, for instance, Bernard of Cluny's understanding when, in the work quoted in the previous essay, he writes:

> O peace; city without time, no praise of thee can go beyond the truth. O dwelling new, the pious company, the pious race, lays thy foundations, carries on the building of thy walls, and brings them to a complete and perfect whole.

For Beatus, the twelve gates of the city are at once the twelve tribes of Israel, the twelve apostles, the twelve prophets, and Christ himself. The Morgan Beatus shows the twelve apostles standing in the gates, each further identified with one of the stones of which the walls are built. The significance of the stones is explained by inscriptions drawn from Isidore of Seville's *Etymologies*. This imagery and its symbolism will be more deeply explored in the following essay; we need only to observe here that the illustration to Beatus' commentary visualizes its metaphor: God's new creation is built up of the individuals who comprise the temple not made by human hands, that is, the Church.

If on the one hand the Heavenly Jerusalem is the Church, understood as the souls of the saints or the body of Christ, on the other, the church as a physical building made by human hands can be seen as a metaphor for the Heavenly Jerusalem. The liturgy for the consecration of a church establishes this association. The text of the Introit for the Mass celebrated in the newly consecrated church building is taken from Genesis (28:17), where Jacob, having seen angels ascending and descending from heaven exclaims: "How awesome is this place! This is none other than the House of God, and this is the gate of heaven." And the epistle read at the consecration Mass is, precisely, the account from the Apocalypse of the descent of the Heavenly Jerusalem. This liturgy assumes, and affirms, that there are indeed places on earth where heaven is revealed and where the creature and creator are together as they will be in the Heavenly Kingdom. Accordingly, a mid-eleventh-century chandelier in a church in Hildesheim, Germany, was inscribed "This is the heavenly city," and we must presume that this belief was widely accepted.

The explicit identification of churches with the Heavenly Jerusalem conferred on them at their consecration makes more meaningful the associations between the Abbey of Cluny and the Heavenly Jerusalem examined in preceding chapters. We have already noted Peter the Venerable's reference to Cluny III as a celestial citadel; Bernard of Cluny's poetic vision of the holy city; and Abbot Odon's characterization of the abbey church (Cluny I) as the monks' "Jerusalem having descended from the heavens." Here it may be added that in his account of the life of St. Hugh, Hildebert, Bishop of Le Mans, France, described Cluny III as "a dwelling place for the glory of God." Its beauty was such, he said, that it seemed suited more to celestial than mortal beings and was called "the angel's walk." These references suggest that the spiritual significance of the physical church as a representation of the Heavenly Jerusalem was at least as prominent to observers in the tenth, eleventh, and early twelfth centuries as was its material form. Painted representations of the Heavenly Jerusalem within churches—those at Saint-Michel-d'Aiguilhe at Le Puy, France (962–984) and San Pietro al Monte at Civate, Italy (eleventh century), for example—could only have augmented this perception. At Cluny itself, the *Maiestas Domini* fresco in the apse and on the west portal tympanum, theophanies drawn from the Apocalypse, fostered the experience of union.

The Heavenly Jerusalem illustrated in the Morgan Beatus (number 1), like that in most of the Beatus manuscripts, is not a temple or church but a city wall. Seen in bird's-eye view, its parts distinguished by color and line and utterly devoid of three-dimensionality, the Heavenly Jerusalem is less depicted than signified. Faithful to the description in the Apocalypse, the city is square in plan, has twelve gates, and is brightly colored. The biblical text describes no buildings within the city, not even a temple, since God the Father and Jesus (the Lamb) were themselves the temple. Indeed, the Morgan Beatus depicts the Lamb holding a cross inside the city. The Heavenly Jerusalem, then, is primarily an architecture of walls and gates: in other words, an exterior, a façade. It has been suggested that the arcaded façades of Romanesque churches, especially in southwest France, can be understood as planar representations of their interiors and that as such they, like the Beatus illustration, should be understood as schematized images of the Heavenly Jerusalem. Thus, returning again to Cluny III, which also had arcades above the western portal, it can be suggested that, together with the great theophanic tympanum, the façade depicted the entire significance of the church. Such imagery would have been recognized, rather than read, by an audience already not only familiar with but also eagerly searching for such associations. It was appropriate, in other words, for the monastic setting, and alluded to that immaterial reality that we know was already present in the mind's eye at Cluny.

So far we have been comparing single buildings—churches—to an entire city. But can a relation be drawn between the medieval city and the Heavenly Jerusalem? It is true that the literary genre of the formal praise of a city (the *laus urbis*) provides little evidence for such a connection. However, in some cases cities (Milan and Florence, for example) were said to have twelve gates in their walls, like the Heavenly Jerusalem, where this was not factually so. And it would seem that the new walls built by Bishop Bernward around Hildesheim in Germany just after the year 1000 really did have twelve gates. Further, a statute of the Italian city of Brescia in 1287 stated explicitly that "the city is made as the model of paradise." Evidence of such connections becomes more abundant as we move forward in time, but it probably would be fair to say that for the centuries with which we are concerned, around the year 1000, before the reawakening of urban society, more thought was given to the associations of churches with the Kingdom of God than to those of cities. It is worth observing that the depictions of architecture in the exhibition (numbers 16, 23, 24, and 28) all show exteriors, and that three of the four depict a city gate flanked by towers. While there is no reason to think that any of these represent the Heavenly Jerusalem (except perhaps by analogy the image of Emmaus, number 16), they bear a formal similarity to the image of the walled city from the Morgan Beatus (number 1). Of course, all of these works draw from well-established conventions of architectural representation. Nonetheless, it is conceivable that the mental image of a city as walls and towers was nourished in this period by a centrally important literary text, the Apocalypse.

The Morgan Beatus was written circa 940–945, probably at the monastery of San Miguel de Escalada near León, Spain; it is signed by Maius. Thus it is to be understood, historically, as representative of a style that owed much to Aragonese King Alfonso III's patronage of monastic art and to the establishment of León as the capital city by his son Ordoño II. The ivory reliquary from León is evidence of the same cultural revival (number 39). Important elements of the style of the Morgan Beatus have been seen as reflecting the Islamic art of southern Spain, especially as practiced in the Caliphate of Cordoba, and are described as "mozarabic" (the art of Spanish Christians during the period of Islamic domination). For example, the horseshoe arches in our illustration have been related to those of the Mosque of Cordoba. However, since such arches are to be found in San Miguel itself (built around 912), Maius may well have drawn from his own monastery church for his image of the Heavenly Jerusalem just as the monks at Cluny drew from theirs. If so, Maius' image would be a painted counterpart to the verbal statements of this analogy from Cluny cited above.

The Morgan depiction of the Heavenly Jerusalem is, for the purposes of our exhibition, an historically appropriate schema for our miniature realization of the city carried out in glass and gemstones and its abstraction as geometry and color (numbers 50 and 51). Like the Morgan Beatus, it calls on the spectator to complete the vision in imagination, since we include but a small samples of the stones of which the whole is built. At the core of John's description, apart from the city's geometry and architectural features (which are supplied by our template, the Morgan Beatus), are images of colored stones and light. For Beatus, light was inherent in the stones and their luminosity depended on no external source. This is the effect that we have tried to embody using design and modern technology. By contrast, we have tried to give some impression of Romanesque architecture through the placement and lighting of the stone sculptures on display. What we hope to have achieved is a visual confrontation between the architecture made by human hands around the year 1000 and the heavenly city of the divine architect that will replace it. Since design has been an important protagonist in articulating the intention of the exhibition, a separate essay is devoted to the installation.

Although the twelve foundation stones of the Heavenly Jerusalem have varying degrees of translucence, all are colorful and light-filled in contrast to the limestone and marble of Romanesque buildings (number 50). Indeed, the gems are the very opposites of stone used for masonry in color, density, and manner of working. (The identification and significance of the twelve gemstones is treated in the next essay.) Whereas the human creations were closely associated with the "measure, number and weight" of the natural world, and were engaged—often explicitly—in weight and support relationships, the Heavenly Jerusalem defies these constraints. The colored stones are infinitely harder, and therefore more durable, than the limestone and marble manipulated by the human architect. What John describes, that massive blocks for foundation walls are made of gemstones, is impossible in nature. John also proposes an architectural paradox in regard to scale, in which the most enormous of all structures, replacing all the existing heavens and earth, is built of materials known only to exist in small samples. In the Heavenly Jerusalem the infinitely large and the infinitely small coincide in a manner that evokes the convergence of opposites, a common definition of God himself. Of course, part of John's intention is to show that the Heavenly City is made of the most precious and costly materials known on earth. But his suggestion results in a reversal of the natural world. Our installation, constrained by the laws of nature, contrasts the tiny gemstones with great architectural masses (numbers 30 and 51). But the mind's eye can reverse this proportional relationship. It is this reversal that we hope to have suggested by confronting the dark, dense matter of human architecture with the pure geometry and color of the immaterial architecture of the Apocalypse (number 50).

> But if only their minds could be seized and held steady, they would be still for a while and, for that short moment, they would glimpse the splendor of eternity which is for ever still. They would contrast it with time, which is never still, and see that it is not comparable. (Augustine, *Confessions* 11:11)

Bibliographic Note

On the Morgan Beatus, see John Williams, *Early Spanish Manuscript Illumination*, New York, 1977, pp. 64–83; and the same author's *The Illustrated Beatus: The Ninth and the Tenth Centuries*, London, 1994. More generally, see Roberto Cassanelli, ed., *Apocalisse: Miniature dal commentario di Beato di Liebana (XI secolo)*, Milan, 1997; Peter K. Klein, "Les Apocalypses romanes et la tradition exégétique," *Cahiers Saint-Michel-de-Cuxa*, 12, 1981, pp. 123–140; and his essay "Les Cycles de L'Apocalypse du haut Moyen Age (IX–XIIIe siècles)," in *L'Apocalypse de Jean. Traditions exégétiques et iconographiques (III–XIIIe siècles)*, Geneva, 1979.

For medieval exegesis, still fundamental is Henri de Lubac, *Medieval Exegesis, 1; The Four Senses of Scripture*, translated by Mark Sebanc and republished in Grand Rapids in 1998 (originally published in 1959).

For notions of Solomon's Temple in our period, see Walter Cahn, "Solomonic Elements in Romanesque Art," in Joseph Gutmann, ed., *The Temple of Solomon. Archeological Fact and Medieval Tradition in Christian, Islamic and Jewish Art*, Missoula, 1976.

The bibliography on the image of God as architect and on the School of Chartres is large. I would cite Katherine Tachau, "God's Compass and *vana curiositas*: Scientific Study in the Old French *Bible Moralisée*," *Art Bulletin*, 80, 1998, pp. 7–33; and J. B. Friedman, "The Architect's Compass in Creation Miniatures of the Later Middle Ages," *Traditio*, 30, 1974, pp. 419–429; M. Ginson, "The Study of the 'Timaeus' in the Eleventh and Twelfth Centuries," *Pensamento*, 25, 1969, pp. 183–194; and Nikolaus Haring, "The Creation and Creator of the World According to Thiery of Chartres and Clarenbaldus of Arras," *Archives d'histoire doctrinale et littéraire du moyen age*, 29, 1955, pp. 137–182.

The relevant texts from the liturgy are conveniently gathered in Laurence H. Stookey, "The Gothic Cathedral as the Heavenly Jerusalem: Liturgical and Theological Sources," *Gesta*, 8, 1969, pp. 35–41.

The quotation from Hildebert of Le Mans is from his *Vita S. Hugonis* 6.39, translated in Ellert Dahl, "*Dilexi decorem domus Dei*. Building to the Glory of God in the Middle Ages," *Acta ad archeologiam et artium historiam pertinentia*, 1, 1981, pp. 157–190.

The suggestion about arcaded church façades is that of Jacques Gardelles in "Recherches sur les origines des façades à étages d'arcatures des églises médiévales," *Bulletin monumentale*, 136, 1978, pp. 113–134.

I extend Flint Schier's observation about spectators' response to pictures to the Romanesque church. *Deeper into Pictures. An Essay on Pictorial Representation*, New York, 1986.

My discussion of Hildesheim is indebted to unpublished research by Steven Scapicchio and James Grisalvi at the Graduate School of Design. Theirs, too, is the association of the text from St. Augustine's *Confessions* with the earthly and heavenly cities.

Material for the comparison between medieval cities and the Heavenly Jerusalem is drawn from Robert Ousterhout, "Flexible Geography and Transportable Topography," *Jewish Art*, 23/24, 1997–1998, pp. 393–404. For the importance of paradox in the idea of the Heavenly Jerusalem, I am indebted to my colleague, Toshiko Mori.

Still very useful for conventions of architectural representation is Paul Lampl, "Schemes of Representation in Early Medieval Art," *Marsyas*, 9, 1961, pp. 6–13.

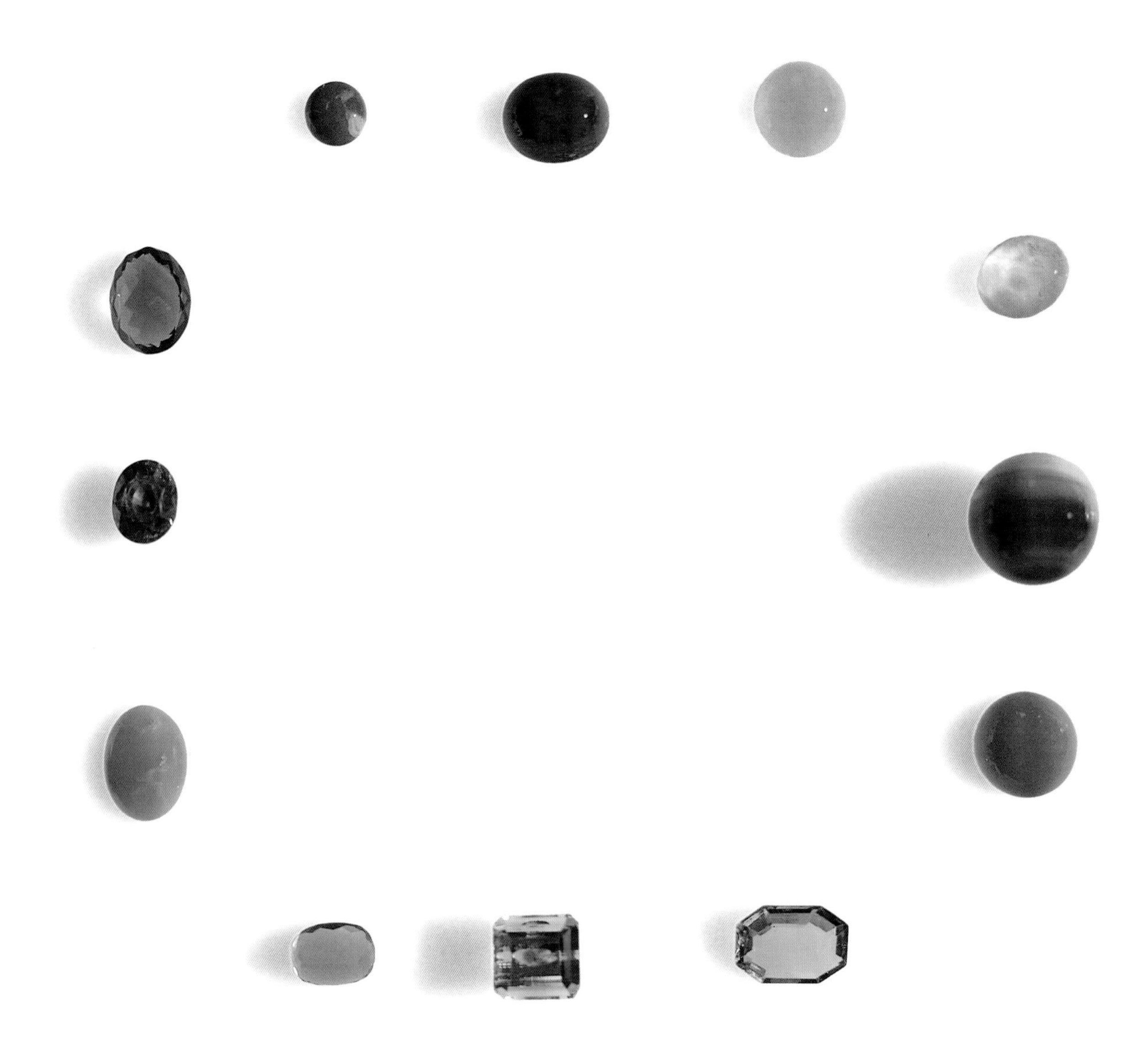

51 The twelve gemstones

the stones of the heavenly jerusalem

HUNTER FORD TURA

While accounts of the Apocalypse have existed since pre-classical times, perhaps the clearest representation of the end of the earthly order, and the subsequent appearance of a heavenly city, comes from St. John's Revelation as set forth in the Bible. In chapter 21, following the description of the various events leading to God's judgment, John described the advent of a new heavenly city that in theological terms is both intense and complex, and, architecturally, is ambiguous at best. While there have been many representations of the Heavenly Jerusalem (most notably the Morgan Beatus manuscript, see number 1), all we know from the textual account is that the city is arranged foursquare, has twelve gates that correspond to the tribes of Israel, and is built on twelve foundation walls made of twelve precious stones.

The idea of a jewel-encrusted heavenly city is not particularly original, as we see similar accounts in the apocryphal book of Tobias, as well as the books of Ezekiel and Daniel. But while there are many existing models, no account is as specific in its identification of the stones as the Apocalypse of John and it is these stones that are the subject of this essay. Its analysis, then, is concerned with three main themes that emerge from John's account. The first involves identifying the stones of the Heavenly Jerusalem, or more specifically, how these stones are classified in both a classical and medieval context, and how we understand them today. The second addresses what each of these stones might mean individually, or rather, what cultural information (i.e., historical, magical, or medicinal properties) is associated with each. Lastly, this essay examines what this group of twelve stones implies or suggests as a whole, attempting to decode chapter 21 of Revelation by identifying what the stones might mean in an allegorical or symbolic context.

To begin with, which stones are mentioned in John's account? Here we are primarily concerned with the Vulgate Bible translated by St. Jerome, as it would have been the version in use in the year 1000. This version states:

> And he carried me away in the spirit to a great and high mountain, and showed me that great city, the holy Jerusalem, descending out of heaven from God, Having the glory of God, radiant as a brilliant light, resembling a very precious gem, like a jasper stone, clear as crystal. It had a great wall and high and it had twelve gates, with the names inscribed thereon, which are the names of the twelve tribes of the children of Israel. On the east there were three gates, on the north three gates, on the south three gates, and on the west three gates. And the wall of the city had twelve foundations, and on them the twelve names of the twelve apostles of the Lamb. And he who talked with me had a measuring rod of golden reed to measure the city and its gates and its wall. And the city was laid foursquare, the length the same as its breadth; and he measured the city with the reed, twelve furlongs, twelve thousand paces. And the length and the breadth and the height were equal. And he measured the wall thereof, a hundred and forty four cubits, according to the measure of a man, that is, of the angel. And the wall was constructed of jasper; and the city itself was pure gold, resembling clear glass. And the foundations of the wall of the city were adorned with all kinds of precious stones. The first foundation was jasper, the second sapphire, the third chalcedony, the fourth emerald, the fifth sardonyx, the sixth sardius, the seventh chrysolite, the eighth beryl, the ninth topaz, the tenth chrysoprasus, the eleventh jacinth, the twelfth amethyst. And the twelve gates were adorned with twelve pearls, one for each of the gates and each gate was made of a single pearl; and the great street of the city was of pure gold, as it were transparent glass. (Apoc. 21:10–21)

52 Jasper

The first stone John mentioned is jasper. An opaque variety of quartz, this stone is found in several colors including red, brown, and green and is commonly located in Italy, Greece, and Egypt. Mineralogists Ruth Wright and Robert Chadbourne (who wrote the book *Gems and Minerals of the Bible* in the early 1970s) feel that the Latin *iaspis* probably refers to a green jasper.

Before examining the specific stones, concentrating on their color, geography, and well-known magical properties, it should be noted that the extent of our historical understanding of these stones—especially in relation to any symbolic meanings—is somewhat limited. First, it is unclear whether John himself understood anything about the supposed powers of precious gems or whether his account should be understood as a revelation of God's prophecy. Secondly, it is more likely that through the study of classical texts, church fathers would have had some knowledge about stones, and therefore would have felt that their inclusion in John's list had a direct symbolic significance that might correspond to God's intentions for a new heavenly order. Lastly, it is important to note that the names of ancient stones are not the same as those of modern stones, creating a good deal of scholarly confusion about the list.

Two surviving classical commentaries are the essential texts in understanding the medicinal or magical characteristics attributed to the precious stones. The first is entitled *On Stones* by Theophrastus, which dates from about 322 B.C. Theophrastus placed jasper in the family of green stones used for cutting seals, which are related to the comparatively rare emerald (*smaragdos*). In fact, Theophrastus thought that the emerald was just a more refined form of the jasper (or rather that the jasper was a "bastard" form of the emerald). The other surviving reference comes from Pliny's *Natural History* (book 37), which dates from the first century A.D. Pliny significantly widened the discussion of jasper, mentioning fourteen separate varieties of *iaspis*, including such obscure variations as the blue jasper. While Pliny's open definition of jasper could serve to confuse modern scholars in determining which stone *iaspis* actually is, medieval writers were able to reach a consensus on the color and nature of the stone.

53 Lapis lazuli

This unanimity certainly comes from the work of Isidore of Seville (ca. 570–636), who in *Etymologies* (book 16) placed the "pine-like" jasper in his discussion of green stones. Hereafter, jasper is almost always referred to as a green stone. This raises an important point about the role of Isidore's text in the year 1000. Indeed, it should be noted that his encyclopedia would have been the main reference for mineralogical matters in a monastic context.

The apocalyptic commentaries of Bede (672/73–735) proposed several magical qualities for jasper, including the notion that the depth of the stone's color had a direct, commensurate relationship to the strength of faith of its holder. Similarly, the belief that jasper commonly signifies an undying faith in Christ, expressed by a green color that never fades, is found in such texts as *On the 12 Stones* (by an unknown medieval author) and in the work of Haymo (d. 855) and Bruno of Asti (1045/49–1123. Marbod of Rennes (1035–1123) suggested that the stone prevents conception, aids childbirth, and keeps the wearer from licentiousness. Likewise, he introduced the notion that jasper ensures a clean life, an idea that resurfaced in thirteenth- and fourteenth-century lapidaries. Lastly, Anselmus of Canturbury (1033–1109) advanced the notion that jasper has the ability to ward off the devil. This is particularly interesting in an eschatological context and may derive from pagan notions of the jasper's repellent qualities. In fact, if we examine the etymology of "jasper" we see that the root *iasp-* is the Greek word for asp, the poisonous snake, which is a reference to the fact that the stone was rumored to keep snakes at bay.

The second stone we are concerned with is *sapphyrios*. While the second foundation of the Heavenly Jerusalem is often mistaken for "sapphire," scholars now believe that the correct translation of the latin *sapphyrus* and the hebrew *sappîr* is, in fact, lapis lazuli. Lapis lazuli is a highly attractive, opaque engraving stone with specks of iron pyrite. This stone has a long history of use in jewelry, and is extremely popular due to its pleasing deep-blue color. Indeed, lapis lazuli was a highly prized stone in antiquity, and had many ceremonial and decorative functions including in jewelry, small statuary, and funerary masks.

Lapis lazuli was mentioned by both Pliny and Theophrastus, and each celebrated its rich, sparkling qualities. The third-century Roman encyclopedist Solinus, ascribed masculine and feminine qualities to the stone. Isidore mentioned *sapphyrios* in his discussions of purple gems, which would seem to reinforce the notion that the stone to which he refers is actually lapis lazuli. Indeed, the rich blue of the stone is much more purple in hue than is the clear blue of the sapphire.

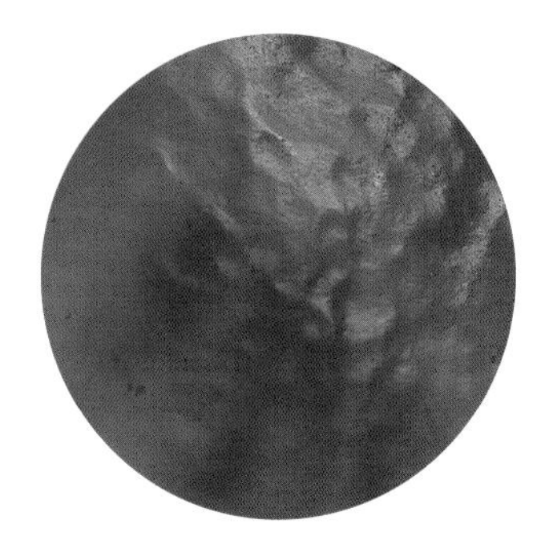

54 Chalcedony

Lapis lazuli was also prized for its magical powers and medicinal uses. Albertus Magnus (ca. 1193–1280), for example, stated that it (*sapphyrios*) cures abscesses and headaches (a power he claimed to have experienced himself), and cools body temperature, although he noted that the stone loses its brilliance once used in the cure of some ailment. In magical terms, lapis lazuli has the property of dispelling sorceries and, perhaps, more importantly, enables necromancers to hear and understand obscure oracles. In a secular context, *Damigeron* asserted that kings wear lapis lazuli around their necks as a defense from harm. This notion was later endorsed by Marbod, who stated that the stone is appropriate for ecclesiastical rings, and by Albertus who mentioned that the stone has an inherent appeal to kings, dukes, and counts—an association that probably derived from the fact that lapis lazuli was commonly set into royal bracelets and necklaces.

John named chalcedony as the substance of the third foundation wall of the Heavenly Jerusalem. This stone is a translucent variety of quartz with a waxy luster. Because of its grayish coloration and materiality, most lapidaries compare chalcedony to a fingernail. The chalcedony is not directly referred to in the work of Pliny, but appears in a larger discussion of onyx (Pliny discussed a variety of onyx from Chalcedon). As a result of the stone's omission from classical sources, chalcedony does not appear in the work of Isidore and many later lapidaries.

55 Emerald

In terms of magical qualities, Pliny believed that if the onyx from Chalcedon were placed under the head of a sleeping man it had the power to show him visions of the future as well as to cure ailments of the eyes. In the apocalyptic context, chalcedony might be understood as a mediator between the earthly and heavenly realms. Albertus Magnus wrote that the stone prevents illusions and melancholy, and preserves the body. In fact, Albertus attested to experiencing these qualities firsthand. Unfortunately, later medieval lapidaries do not offer much more information about the magical properties of the stone. The twelfth-century poem *Canticum*, for example, merely states that chalcedony "represents a strong faith" and is "very popular among the people." Also worthy of mention, the writings of both Marbod and *Damigeron* suggest that the color of the stone changes after it has been handled, and this fading of intensity reflects the diminishing of its perceived magical qualities.

The fourth stone John mentioned is the emerald, or the Latin *smaragdus,* a highly esteemed stone due to its rich green color. Theophrastus broadly defined *smaragdus* as any green stone (or rock) including green marble, alabaster, or even green glass, but most scholars are confident that in this biblical context *smaragdus* almost certainly refers to the emerald. Pliny praised the stone for its attractive qualities, remarking that no other shade of green is as pleasant to the eye. Isidore did not greatly expand on Pliny's assessment, but Albertus Magnus poetically described the stone's color, which "seems to tinge the air around it with its own greenness."

Albertus claimed that the emerald increases the wealth of the wearer, strengthens weak sight, and has the power to cure epilepsy. The most entertaining characteristic he related is that the emerald inclines the wearer toward chastity because the stone cannot withstand sexual intercourse. He even gave the example of a king of Hungary who wore this stone on his finger when he had intercourse with his wife, and as a result, the stone was broken into three pieces.

56 Sardonyx

57 Sard (Carnelian)

The fifth wall of the city's foundation is made up of the sardonyx stone, a combination of onyx and sard. The stone has flat parallel stripes of two or three different colors, which results in a fine layering of contrasting colors, and is found primarily in Egypt and India. Although there is not a great deal of symbolic importance linked to the sardonyx, the stone was considered a gem of great value in classical times. In fact, it was a common practice among lawyers striving to appear prosperous to rent the costly sardonyx rings that signified an extravagant mode of living. This may be related to the rumor that sardonyx was the favorite stone of the Emperor Claudius and was quite fashionable in Rome after its introduction to the city by Africanus the Elder. Its association with opulence, and the fact that sardonyx stones could be quite large, may be significant in John's description of the Heavenly Jerusalem. Indeed, the larger the specimen, the more dramatic and beautiful the coloration of the banding pattern. Sardonyx, then, might have joined John's list based on its earthly associations with wealth and power. Medieval texts, however, present a more somber image of the stone. Albertus Magnus, for example, tells us that the sardonyx makes a man simple and chaste and the twelfth-century lapidaries refer to the stone's red color as representing the blood of the martyrs.

The sixth stone of the Heavenly Jerusalem is the "sard," which is also called carnelian. The stone's deep-orange to brownish-red color can be improved by heat treatment, and in classical times carnelian was commonly used in headdresses, capes, and jewelry. Pliny tells us that there was no gem more esteemed: it was even used in the treatment of King Tut's tomb. The carnelian's associations with both wealth and royalty may be significant in the biblical context as a way of reinforcing God's judgment over all in the Heavenly Jerusalem.

In terms of magical and medicinal qualities, medieval texts note that the carnelian brings joy to the individual, and makes the wearer well received wherever he or she goes. Albertus Magnus wrote that the stone protects against incantations and sorcery, sharpens the wits of the wearer, and has the power to drive away bad dreams. The most entertaining property of the carnelian, however, comes from Marbod, who made the bizarre claim that carrying twenty pounds of grain and a carnelian stone prevents the wearer from seeing evil things.

58 Chrysolite (Peridot)

59 Beryl (Aquamarine)

The seventh stone of the foundation is the chrysolite, which most likely refers to the modern peridot. There is no consensus, however, on the specific stone mentioned in John's account because "chrysolite" (our peridot) and "topaz" were used interchangeably in classical descriptions. This confusion certainly dates back at least to Pliny, who wrote of a stone called *topazios* that came from the island of Topazos in the Red Sea. Ironically, no topaz has ever been found on the island, the world's principal provider of peridot.

It would seem unlikely, given that the topaz is mentioned as the substance of the ninth foundation wall of the Heavenly Jerusalem, that a stone would be repeated in John's sequence. This coloration would be reinforced by Isidore's description of the stone as "golden." In terms of magical properties of the peridot, we learn from Albertus Magnus that the stone has the ability to ease breathing, to drive away terrors, melancholy, and phantasms, and to expel stupidity. To maximize these powers, however, Albertus stated the stone must be set in gold. The twelfth-century *Canticum* states that the brightness of the stone is meant to reflect the radiance of the divine and can even light a dark room.

The eighth foundation wall is made of beryl, specifically the aquamarine variety that comes from Spain and India. Beryl was one of the most valuable stones of antiquity. Indeed, the classification refers to a much larger family of stones that includes the emerald. Pliny and later Isidore wrote that beryl has the "same nature" as the emerald, clearly reinforcing this familial connection. The beryl can cure sicknesses of the liver and prevent shortness of breath, as well as prevent belching and watery eyes. It has two very interesting social qualities that are specifically discussed in the work of Albertus Magnus: the power to prevent sloth, and to promote agreement between husband and wife.

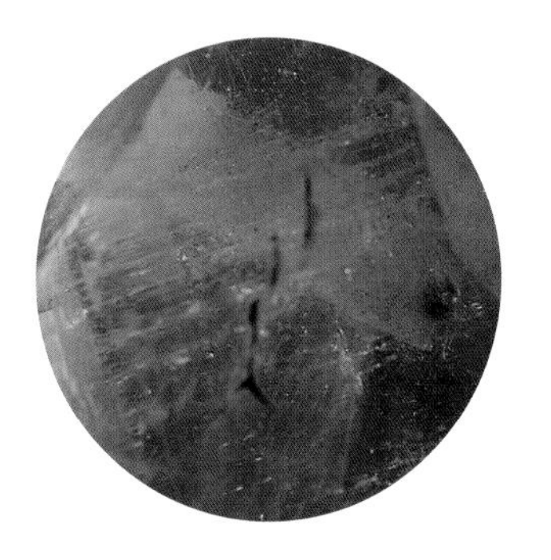

60 Topaz

61 Chrysophase

As mentioned, in regard to the conflation of the terms "chrysolite" and "topaz," the ninth stone of the heavenly Jerusalem is probably the topaz. A yellow or red stone (although Isidore mentioned it in his description of green gems), it is commonly found in Ethiopia and parts of Asia. Albertus stated that the topaz could prevent boils, cure hemorrhoids, and prevent lunacy. Other medieval writing claimed that wearing the topaz is proof that the wearer loves the Church, and it ensures charity and chastity.

The tenth stone mentioned in John's account is the chrysoprase. Etymologically, the stone's name (*chrysos-* means "golden" and *-prason* means "leek") indicates its unique golden-green coloration. Chrysoprase comes primarily from Ethiopia and its value and desirability depend on the brilliance of its color, which decreases when the stone is exposed to heat and light. Neither Theophrastus nor Pliny ever mentioned chrysoprase specifically by name, but rather grouped it into the larger classification of jasper. Isidore, on the other hand, mentioned the *chrysoprasus* in his description of fire-colored stones.

Albertus Magnus also mentioned the stone, and suggested that it has talismanic qualities and affords the power of impunity in criminal situations. Indeed, if a thief was sentenced to be hanged or beheaded, by placing this stone in his mouth he would immediately escape from his executioners. This effect is probably related to the notion that the stone has the power to make one invisible. Only a few medieval texts attribute symbolic properties to the stone, however. The *Alphabetical Lapidary* and the *Lapidaire Chrétien* (twelfth century) say virtually nothing on the matter, a historiographical byproduct of its omission in classical sources.

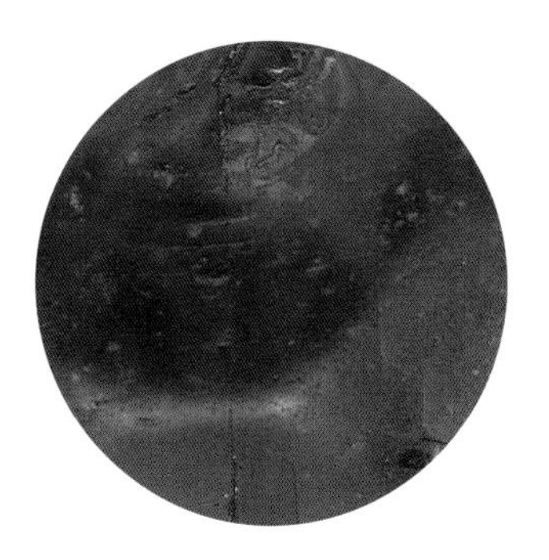

62 Jacinth

The eleventh stone in the walls of the Heavenly Jerusalem is the jacinth, or the Latin *hyacinthus*. In modern terms, *hyacinthus* is used interchangeably with the term jacinth and refers to a brownish stone that comes from Ethiopia. Pliny likened the *hyacinthus* to the amethyst except for its slightly paler color, like a hyacinth flower "fading away." In the third century, Solinus picked up on this theme when he described *hyacinthus* as a violet or blue stone with a "watery" appearance. These classical assessments of the stone influenced Isidore and later medieval lapidarists.

As with the chrysolite and topaz, there is good deal of controversy surrounding which stone is meant in John's account. The Vulgate of St. Jerome refers to this stone as *hyacinthus*, which could have one of two meanings. The first possibility is that *hyacinthus* refers to a blue stone, perhaps the modern sapphire, which was the common association during biblical times. Wright and Chadbourne are certain on this point, and wrote, "After reading the translations of the same verse there can be little doubt that hyacinth, jacinth and sapphire all refer to a blue gemstone." Indeed, the Greek *huakinthos* and the Latin *hyacinthus* both are references to the color blue. This is reinforced in certain biblical translations, most notably the *Jerusalem Bible*, in which Rev. 9:17 reads:

> I saw the horses and those who sat on them, and they had breastplates of flame color, hyancinth-blue and sulphur-yellow.

Indeed, *hyacinthos* mentioned by Pliny is definitely a blue gem and Solinus, similarly, thought it referred to a blue sapphire. Modern mineralogists such as Kunz and Burnham, however, feel that the jacinth in the Heavenly Jerusalem was a "rich crimson." Therefore, we are left with a stalemate in which the classical and medieval texts suggest one color for the biblical stone and modern historians propose another.

63 Amethyst

The twelfth stone, of the final foundation wall, is amethyst. The amethyst is a clear lavender-to-bluish-violet crystal quartz with varying degrees of color intensity. In fact, it is basically a rock crystal colored purple by deposits of iron, and is considered one of the most attractive of all gems. The amethyst discussed in classical texts usually came from India. In historiographical terms, amethyst is the only gem to appear in the account of the Heavenly Jerusalem that is common to all of the major versions of the Bible. As such, there can be little doubt that modern amethyst was the stone that John mentioned in Revelation.

According to Hebrew folklore, amethyst induced pleasant dreams. Greek tradition held that it could prevent drunkenness. While both Pliny and Theophrastus mentioned these qualities (Pliny disagreed), it is not immediately clear how these secular associations might be significant in our understanding of the Heavenly Jerusalem (however in the case of the latter it provides any number of speculative possibilities). In medieval texts, the Venerable Bede mentioned that the amethyst represents the justice of man, and Albertus Magnus wrote that it represses evil thoughts, confers a good understanding of what is knowable, and assists the hunter in his pursuit of wild animals.

After examining the individual character of the stones of the Heavenly Jerusalem, what do they suggest or imply as a group? Or rather, how does an understanding of these twelve stones overall affect our reading of John's account of the Apocalypse, or better our understanding of the medieval conception of the heavenly city?

To address these questions, consider the physical characteristics of the twelve stones in John's account. First, there is the issue of color, which we should understand to be outside the experience of most people who heard or read the words of John in the Middle Ages. Indeed, other than colors' presence in nature (also one of God's creations), only imperial or clerical figures with jeweled crowns and garments would have been a main reference point for vibrant colors. This is important in two ways: first, it makes the strong connection between color and authority, which clearly assigns color to a realm outside the daily experience of most common people; second, as an expression of God's glory and wrath in Revelation, the stones transcend any mere secular ostentation, and through the transfer of power, the image of an intensely colored city expands the limits of the imagination.

The second physical characteristic of note is the stones' materiality, and in this case I mean their relative transparency or opacity as well as their relative hardness. We should envision the heavenly city as aglow with the light of God's truth and we can certainly imagine this light shining from these crystalline walls in quite an impressive fashion. Perhaps the most important physical trait of these walls is that they are vast, and beyond human comprehension. While their actual dimensions are unclear, the city's walls are sublimely immense.

It is also important to recognize the thematic nature of the stones' groupings. We know that secular constructions like "wealth" and "power" do not exist in the Heavenly Jerusalem, given St. Augustine's reminder that there can be no sin in the City of God, for the "corruptible elements" have been judged and cast into the eternal fire. The vast wealth of riches represented by the precious stones is only significant when compared to earthly standards of wealth. As noted before, in most cases these stones have very close associations with secular power and royalty. Yet due to their size, the bejeweled walls of the heavenly city are more impressive than any riches a secular authority could hope to accumulate. Emeralds, for example, almost certainly would have been included by John for both their beauty and rarity, and an entire foundation wall built of emerald should not be seen as insignificant. Here again, the stones as a group should be understood as a testament to the exalted nature of God's power. Furthermore, many of the stones in the Heavenly Jerusalem have associations with nativity, evoking the notion of rebirth and God's deliverance from original sin.

In contrast to those cultural associations that relate to the twelve as a single entity, other interpretations concern the individual stone's position. An example of this is a statement common in many medieval texts: "Jasper signifies Christ." It clearly suggests a conscious hierarchical arrangement. In this case, the stone has an individual meaning, possibly operating independently of the other stones.

These symbolic interpretations, which come to us mostly from the Latin fathers, include the use of numerology. One numerological interpretation comes from Andreas, who specified an apostle to each stone: jasper=Peter, sapphire=Paul, chrysoprase=Thaddeus, etc. In this case, twelve stones = twelve apostles. Other related possibilities of this type are the correlation between the twelve stones and the twelve months, the twelve steps of Jacob's Ladder, and the twelve tribes of Israel.

Another symbolic interpretation based on number has to do with the order in which the stone appears. For example, jasper as the first foundation symbolizes Christ; lapis (*sapphyrios*) as the second foundation represents man's covenant with God (two parts); chalcedony as the third foundation represents the trinity (three parts); emerald as the fourth foundation represents the four evangelists; chrysolite, which is the seventh stone, represents the seven gifts of the Holy Ghost, and so on. In this case, there is a correspondence between the number in the order, and the number of parts in the represented object. This interpretation, of course, raises questions about the order in which the stones are presented.

There is another possible interpretation, which may never be fully developed due to the confusion about the specificity of the stones in John's list. It involves the possibility of an acrostic structure contained within the name of each stone, each tribe, apostle, and so forth. This interpretive strategy, however, is mere speculation and depends on the historiographical certainty of each stone, something scholars may never be able to achieve.

Even if there were a conscious symbolic superstructure in the writing of John (for example, God knew about the powers of the stones, or John's intent was to invoke a larger set of issues in his account), these twelve stones of the Heavenly Jerusalem inspired awe in the medieval mind as they operated on several associative levels simultaneously. Certainly, the medieval mind would have been able to freely sample meanings, based on what individuals knew about each stone in any of the overlapping contexts of medicine, politics, and folklore. Perhaps, then, it is the earthly associations and not the post-apocalyptic conditions that are important in our interpretation. In the end, the true significance of the stones is the ability for their powerful imagery to slide across a range of cultural associations—many fraught with supernatural power, social stratification, and perhaps even physical pain—activating a response of awe at the prospect of the end of the earthly order and the advent of God's judgment.

Sources

Albertus Magnus (translation by Dorothy Wycoff), *Book of Minerals* (Oxford: Clarendon Press, 1967).

Isidori Hispalensis Episcopi, *Etymologarum Sine Originum, Tomus II, Libros XI–XX* (Oxford: Oxford University Press, 1911).

George Frederick Kunz, *The Curious Lore of Precious Stones* (Philadelphia and London: J. B. Lippincott Company, 1913).

Caius Plinus Secundus (notes and translation by John Bostock and H. T. Riley), *Natural History, Book XXXVI* (London: Henry G. Bohn, 1857).

Caius Julius Solinus (translation by Arthur Golding), *Collectanea rerum memorabilium* (Gainesville: Scholars' Facsimiles & Reprints, 1955).

Theophrastus (edited, with introduction, translation, and commentary by D. E. Eichholz), *De lapidibus.* (Oxford: Clarendon Press, 1965).

Ruth V. Wright and Robert L. Chadbourne, *Gems and Minerals of the Bible* (New York: Harper & Row 1970).

observations on architectural photography

JAMES ACKERMAN

The achievement of successful photographic processes during the 1830s (presented to the public in 1839) by Louis-Jacques-Mandé Daguerre and Hippolite Bayard in France and by William Henry Fox Talbot in England radically affected all fields in which the image played an important role, and none more than the study of architecture. Talbot's technique, based on the production of a paper negative from which large numbers of positive prints could be made, was more effective in providing widespread access to visual information than Daguerre's, which, while realizing a significantly greater precision of detail by the exposure of the object directly onto a silver-plated metal ground, was limited to unique positive images. In the early years of photography, when long exposures were required, architecture and landscape subjects were favored partly because they did not move, but also because they satisfied a growing interest in the world beyond everyday experience, manifested as well in an increase in travel—previously the prerogative of a privileged minority—among the middle classes. Talbot capitalized on this feature of his work by publishing books of photographic prints (e.g., *Sun Pictures of Scotland*, 1845)—initially called Talbotypes but soon known as Calotypes—that appealed to the current culture of Romanticism and to the proponents of medieval revival, depicting castles, ruined abbeys, ancient country houses, and the undisturbed moors and downs celebrated by Wordsworth and Sir Walter Scott.

Talbot wrote in 1839, "In the summer of 1835 I made in this way [i.e., with the use of small *camerae obscurae* and short focal-length lenses] a great number of representations of my house in the country, which is well suited to the purpose, from its ancient and remarkable architecture. And this building I believe to be the first that was ever yet known to have drawn its own picture." Like many early photographers, Talbot, a mathematician who kept in close contact with the scientific community, was unaware of—or unwilling to admit—the extent to which photographic images cannot simply be represented as reflections of reality, but must depend on various elements of choice (of subject, position, framing, lighting, focus, etc.) and must reflect and address the ideology and taste of their time. Nonetheless, he must have appreciated the degree to which the techniques of photography themselves imposed certain expressive results—for example, the speed of exposure, the focal length of lenses, the graininess resulting from the use of paper negatives.

Interest in Romantic and medieval subject matter had been nurtured by books and paintings since the beginning of the nineteenth century. Large-scale, often multi-volume publications on medieval architecture with engraved illustrations and extensive historical and descriptive texts were widely available in England and France. Augustus Charles Pugin, father of the influential spokesman for the Gothic Revival, Augustus Welby N. Pugin, devoted his career to such publication (e.g., *The Architectural Antiquities of Normandy*, 1827–1828). Illustrations of this type established conventions of architectural representation that were adopted, no doubt unconsciously, by photographers: the positions from which to shoot the façades and apsidal ends of churches, the interiors, the choice of details. The engravings were of necessity more interpretative than early photographs: the technique of engraving, which required carving fine lines into metal plates, could not convey the nuanced effects of light and shade available to the photographer, and the style and "hand" of the engraver exerted a greater influence on the way the object was interpreted than did the disposition of the photographer—at least in the "documentary" style of early photographic surveys. On the other hand, the camera had—and still has—limitations that did not affect the draftsman: it could not, for example, capture the whole of a church façade with its towers, or an interior with its vaults, without distortion due to the nature of the lens, especially in sites cramped by surrounding buildings (the engraver could simply eliminate irrelevant obstructions at will), and it could not, prior to the invention of artificial illumination, capture ornamental and structural detail in poorly lit places. In the end, both techniques were profoundly affected by convention and manner; they involve misrepresentation as well as representation. The photograph prevailed over the engraving, however, because it could be produced and distributed more rapidly (and hence in greater quantity), more cheaply, and by practitioners less arduously trained.

It is impossible for these reasons to distinguish clearly a "documentary" style of early architectural photographs from an interpretative one, yet some distinctions are warranted. Many photographers were engaged, particularly in France and England, to carry out programs documenting national monuments, and in one case, that of Edouard Baldus, to provide a survey of structures serving the national railway system. Since the purpose was to assemble archives of permanent relevance, the photographer was obliged to restrain as far as possible personal inclination in order to appeal to the taste of his time. The same would have been true of many of the photographs of monuments and frequented sites made commercially for mass distribution, which tended to repress idiosyncratic approaches in order to attract a variety of buyers. At the same time, other photographers became conscious of the aesthetic potential of the medium and portrayed architecture expressively, often inspired by painting (in England, especially the work of Turner). Between these extremes fall photographs intended to convey the actuality of buildings by focusing on aspects such as massing, modulation of light and shadow, texture, relations to the surrounding physical context, and so forth.

The two functions of the architectural photograph most relevant to the present exhibition are its use by the historian of architecture and architectural sculpture and by the architect as a resource in designing new buildings employing reference to historical styles.

For the architectural designer, photographs can provide a rich resource and stimulus. The fact that photography became available at the height of the medieval revival and of the taste for the "picturesque" made this especially evident.

In contrast, architects working in the earlier classical revival style (which continued to be practiced alongside the medieval revival) found measured plans and elevations in the tradition of Stuart and Revett's *The Antiquities of Athens* (1762) more useful than photographs, because the strict rules of classical composition and proportions could be conveyed more effectively in plans and elevations. Medieval revival and picturesque architecture emphasized pictorial effects of massing, contrasts of light and shadow, texture and color, richness of ornament, all of which could be captured more effectively by the camera than by the draughtsman and engraver. Potentialities for early architectural photography were suggested during the first three decades of the nineteenth century by new techniques of printing, the lithograph, the aquatint, and the mezzotint, which were employed increasingly to convey these aspects of architecture, and were the principle vehicles for the diffusion of the picturesque—a style initially stimulated by landscape painting (e.g., J. B. Papworth, *Rural Residences*, 1813, a book of models of dwellings in the rustic style).

Photographs provided a resource that not only expanded the designer's knowledge of familiar historical traditions but also extended the scope of his knowledge to a wide spectrum of historical styles less accessible at first hand, especially those of Egypt, Byzantium, and the Middle East. In France, the influential Second Empire style promoted by the École des Beaux-Arts employed a rich amalgam of ancient, Renaissance, Baroque, and Rococo elements and ornamental motifs that made a photographic archive a virtual necessity for the practitioner.

In the second half of the nineteenth century, architects increasingly became the patrons of photographers as it became evident that photographic portfolios could serve as a way of attracting clients. Henry Hobson Richardson must have sponsored or at least encouraged photographic campaigns surveying his major buildings and published in the *Monographs of American Architecture* (1886) and in Mrs. Schuyler van Rensselaer's *Henry Hobson Richardson and His Architecture* (1888).

Toward the end of the century innovative photographers (such as Frederick H. Evans, Edward Steichen, Alfred Stieglitz) turned away from a documentary approach and employed architectural subjects in the expression of a distinct personal style. Documentary photography became less experimental and varied. In the new modernist architecture of the early twentieth century, images of historical architecture were less useful to the designer, but photographs of contemporary work, particularly those of the most eminent architects, powerfully affected the spread of the style.

Photographs are fundamental to the practice of historical research and interpretation because they can provide the scholar with an almost infinitely expandable collection of visual records of buildings and details of buildings in his/her area of research. While there can be no effective substitute for experiencing buildings at first hand, our memory is incapable of storing all of the visible aspects of any one, much less the entire achievement of a particular body of work. The beginnings of the modern discipline of architectural history—and the history of the other visual arts—can be traced roughly to the period of early photography. Perhaps under the influence of the taxonomic method in science (e.g., in the botany of Linnaeus and others) scholars classified works of art according to style—the style of a historical period, a nation, an area, an individual designer. This could be done only by the method of comparison—establishing a class of production through the determination of common traits among different objects. Comparative judgments with respect to style were also necessary to support a narrative of evolutionary change that already had been a feature of literary and art criticism in antiquity and the Renaissance. To this end, photographs became indispensable in ways that drawings and engravings could not be; in consulting a graphic work we have no way of determining how accurately and with what emphasis it represents the object, while the photograph, though by no means a transparent rendition of the object, contains clues as to its degree of documentary reliability.

Two of the individuals represented in the exhibition, H. H. Richardson and Arthur Kingsley Porter, were profoundly affected and sustained by photographs, the one in his practice as an architect, the other in his study of Romanesque sculpture and architecture and monuments of Celtic art.

Richardson was an undergraduate at Harvard from 1856 to 1859 and in 1860 enrolled in the École des Beaux-Arts in Paris, where he studied sporadically for the ensuing five years, returning to the United States in 1865. He amassed a collection of over 3,000 photographs of European architecture (now preserved in the Special Collections division in the Frances Loeb Library of the Graduate School of Design at Harvard) in the last years of the nineteenth century, primarily of the Romanesque period, which he was the first major architect to turn to as a source of design inspiration (numbers 18, 19, 20, 21, and 22). Few if any of the photographs in the archive appear to date from before his time in Paris; the bulk were acquired after his return from Paris in 1865 and on his visit to Europe in 1882.

So far as can be deduced from the photographs themselves, Richardson was more interested in the documentary value of the prints than in their quality; in the case of provincial examples of medieval architecture he often may have had no choice, having to depend on the work of local photographers, whose business probably was based on portraiture and wedding pictures. Perhaps many of these were made expressly for him; some of the documentation of cloister sculptures seems too inept to have been offered on the open market. As Richardson was also an avid collector of architectural books, it is not always possible to distinguish instances of the use of photographs from the use of book illustrations as stimuli for his designs. As expected, the bulk of the prints are of French and Italian Romanesque ecclesiastical subjects, but Islamic, Asian, Moorish, and Renaissance buildings also appear. Gothic architecture is almost as frequently represented as Romanesque, particularly that of France and England. Among the English acquisitions is a suite of large prints by the brilliant mid-century British photographer Roger Fenton (1818–1891).

Richardson's use of photographs in the process of design is likely seen in the crossing tower of Trinity Church in Boston (1872–1877), which is derived from that of the Cathedral of Salamanca; a story was told that a photograph of the crossing tower, which was given to the architect by John La Farge, was passed on to Richardson's assistant, Stanford White (later a principal in the firm of McKim, Mead and White), to produce a working drawing. The entrance porch of Austin Hall at Harvard is an adaptation from those of churches of southern France, particularly the one at St. Gilles-du-Gard. But for the most part, Richardson's references to the period are to be found more in the use of polychromy and rugged texture in masonry, sculptural detail, particularly in capitals, and in the massing of elements, as in the combination of the vertical emphasis of a tower in relation to the horizontal disposition of the body of a building; such characteristics would have been culled from a variety of visual sources.

Kingsley Porter, the great scholar of medieval art, took thousands of photographs himself or with the help of assistants under his direction. Many of his interests would not have been represented in commercially available photographs. His archive, preserved in the Visual Studies division of the Fine Arts Library, is primarily devoted to architecture, sculpture, and manuscript illumination in France, Spain, and Italy, with a group documenting Celtic sculpture; it includes a large body of negatives, presumably taken by him, as well as prints purchased to supplement his own work (numbers 36, 37, 38, 39, and 40). The fact that his most influential publication, *Romanesque Sculpture of the Pilgrimage Roads* (1923) was accompanied by nine volumes of photographs from his archive illustrates his conviction that scholarship in his field had to be grounded in images. The varying sizes of negatives indicate that he employed several different cameras. The smaller ones suggest that he made extensive use of the commercial snapshot camera (Kodak) developed by Eastman and other manufacturers at the close of the nineteenth century. The photographs taken by Kingsley Porter are not of professional quality, but they served as notes and reminders of what he had seen and studied; he did not supplement them with drawings.

For both architects and scholars interested in the arts of the Romanesque period, the photograph became an essential tool because surviving monuments were not concentrated in urban centers or even restricted regions, but were in such diverse locations that one could have a firsthand acquaintance with only a portion of them.

Author's note

I am indebted to Ralph Lieberman for insights into the limits of representation in architectural photography.

Gallery vestibule and entrance wall evoking Romanesque style

the installation a question of meaning and representation

MARCO STEINBERG

REPRESENTATION

Exhibition design has always had to grapple with the fundamental problem of representation. On the one hand there are absolute "truths" about artifacts (the "thing" out there), on the other there are relative values for which the artifact stands. This question of value becomes fundamentally a question of representation—how to represent that which is not inextricably bound to the artifact. And to answer, one must also negotiate a question of abstraction—how can the elements of an exhibition suggest that which is absent while clearly representing that absence?

Presentation, representation, and abstraction are tied to the discourse of meaning in the display of artifacts. Meaning in an exhibition of artifacts resides within a complex array of factors. In the capital from the abbey of Dommartin, for example, meaning resides within the properties that are directly tied to the physical artifact (it made is of stone), properties that are indirectly tied to the artifact (the impetus for and place of creation), the context in which it is displayed (a museum), and the presence of a viewer.

Furthermore, there are objects displayed, such as drawings or photographs, which are physical representations of the artifact. These secondary sources have qualities and values in and of themselves. Thus the meaning of any artifact resides in the complex interplay between its direct and indirect properties and the viewer. Further complicating the matter, this set of relationships is in constant flux, never fixed.

SCULPTURE AND ARCHITECTURE

One could argue that an artifact is transformed into sculpture by the base on which it is displayed. A base (understood as a neutral ground that enables a separation between object and background) allows the artifact to be appreciated and understood as independent from the physicality of its support. The artifact is transformed into sculpture by the emergence of a new background (the base) and a foreground (the object). However, when dealing with artifacts that belong within a context of architecture, the operation is different. Rather than claim difference or autonomy, the artifact of architecture represents—much like a swatch of fabric—a system, a continuity.

In the exhibition design, the intent was to provide a reading of the artifact as representative of an architectural fabric that suggested continuity, scale, and relative value between the various pieces, while at the same time suggesting a separation between the implied architecture and the architecture of the gallery.

Two distinct elements that could be understood both as an architecture (in terms of scale and space-making ability) and as a base (by distinguishing between itself and the architecture of the gallery) were developed: an eight-foot band of gray paint and columnar-like wall protrusions. Both architectures/bases would inextricably bind to the logic of the gallery walls, yet be read independently of it.

Installation with visualizations of the end of time, lefthand wall

The paint, by virtue of its scale and wrapping of multiple surfaces, developed a secondary spatial reading within the gallery. It also provided continuity and defined a space for the objects. This paint mask also established a background that enabled artifacts to be understood as clearly "hanging" within the gallery.

The wall protrusions, by virtue of their scale and paternity to the gallery walls, developed secondary spatial readings both in and distinct from the gallery. The symmetrical disposition and proximity to the corners, also helped create a secondary spatial reading of a niche.

Capitals placed on top of the columnar protrusions appeared in an abstracted, relative position and scale, as one might have found in the original cathedral. The capitals would thus become part of the architectural experience of the gallery. But because they clearly are not part of the abstracted white bases that support them, the capitals also become sculptures within the gallery.

THE GALLERY

The exhibition occupies a small portion of the museum's second floor: a room and a terminal wing of the loggia. Tucked deep within the envelope of the museum, the space did not present inherent, clear boundaries that would enable the exhibition to have unity, to be a cohesive whole. Questions of presence, entrance, and continuity within the exhibition therefore became critical in the design.

Because the exhibition was not large enough to clearly have an identity of its own, clarity of boundaries and scale were needed to allow the exhibition to have a life independent of the museum structure.

In defining boundaries, consideration had to be given to the entrance (as a moment of passing-through, as a threshold) and techniques that could allow for difference to coexist within the context of the institution. The hallway, for example, had to have several clear readings: it had to be part of the larger museum, it had to signal the entrance to this specific exhibition, and it had to show a clear allegiance with the rest of the exhibition. This was done through the placement of exhibition elements (such as the entrance corbel) and architecture. The exhibition items were placed in ways that defined frontage (in the entrance to the exhibition) and multi-axial relationships (to turn the entrance axis to that of the gallery beyond).

Gallery center: the case enclosing the 12 gemstones

Romanesque carvings (righthand wall) set in architectural context

THE EXHIBITION

Within the main room there is an apparently symmetrical and central disposition of elements. At the center of the gallery is a wooden, glass-topped case that encloses the precious jewels—each symbolizing a different foundation wall of the Heavenly Jerusalem. Glowing in the precisely focused light sources, these small gems acquire great presence. With the entrance to one's back, on the right is a large mural abstracting the inherent geometry of the Heavenly Jerusalem, which allows viewers not only to locate and identify the gems, but also to understand the gems as the representation of these foundations.

On the opposite wall carved artifacts are affixed to a columnar wall surface. The juxtaposition of the two walls begins to set up the tension between the earthly makings and the representation of the divine, between artifact and representation. Along the back wall runs the series of prints, representations by Odilon Redon of St. John's vision of the Apocalypse. Facing this series, a pair of corbels on both sides of the entrance brackets the door, and once again, into the architecture of the room.

Organizing the interplay of artifact and representation is the central disposition of the glowing gems and the use of the continuous painted band on the wall. The color band provides a background to the drawings and links those walls to the walls of artifacts. Outside the gallery, the hallway space serves to reorient the circulation axis, from that of the museum loggia to the room. The columnar support from the Monastery of San Pelayo Antealtares stands in the midst of it, becoming a visible icon, a suggestion, of the meaning of the exhibition within.

The central questions—of representation and artifact, of architecture and the representation of architecture—became both resistance and structure in the organization of the exhibition. The use and disposition of symmetry, banding, and folding pigmented surfaces, scale and placement between display items, lighting, walls, and bases, all enabled difference to coexist within a whole perceived by viewers as teetering between a space of architecture and a space of exhibition.

on the study of early medieval art at harvard

JAMES ACKERMAN

Study of the art of the Middle Ages was supported to a much greater degree in the earliest university departments and programs of the history of art in this country than it is today. The first Harvard professor—and perhaps the first professor in the country—to have taught the history of art (apart from instruction by artists in art schools and departments), Charles Eliot Norton, whose initial teaching at Harvard was in temporary positions in literature, concentrated on the medieval and early Renaissance periods, particularly in Italy. Norton invited Charles Herbert Moore, who had been employed by the University as a teacher of studio art in the scientific school, to join him in teaching history, and Moore later published books on Gothic and Renaissance architecture. Harvard's first scholar of medieval art of international reputation was Arthur Kingsley Porter, who made the most impressive contributions of his generation in America to the knowledge of Romanesque architecture and sculpture in the years preceding and following World War I. His student, Kenneth J. Conant, devoted a large part of his academic life to the excavation and reconstruction (in drawings and models) of the huge French Abbey and Church of Cluny, destroyed in the French Revolution. Ernst Kitzinger, on his appointment as the first holder of the University professorship named for Arthur Kingsley Porter, came to Cambridge to teach on a regular basis after many years at Dumbarton Oaks Center for Early Christian and Byzantine Studies. He inaugurated the program in late antique and early medieval art, expanding the sphere of investigation eastward and to an earlier time.

CHARLES ELIOT NORTON

Charles Eliot Norton (1827–1908) was a towering figure in the Harvard community of the later nineteenth century, a person of impressive gifts as a literary and cultural critic whose extensive knowledge of the European heritage qualified him to publish admired studies on Dante, Goethe, Carlyle, Walter Scott, Emerson, and the art of Greece and the Middle Ages and Renaissance. He received his bachelor's and master's degrees at Harvard and served as an instructor of French in 1851. In 1863–1864 he was appointed University lecturer on the medieval revival of learning, and in 1874 was first given a professorial appointment as professor of the history of the arts, a position from which he retired in 1898. He believed that the study of the arts was the chief defense against what he considered to be the increasing barbarism of modern society, particularly in America—to the point of his questioning the validity of democracy. Norton's cultural credo is summarized in a sentence from a lecture on the role of the fine arts (1889): "the fine arts are the only real test of the spiritual qualities of a race and the standard by which ultimately its share in the progress of humanity must be measured, for they are the permanent expression of its soul; of the desires and aspirations by which it has been inspired...the best that a people has to express will be expressed in its fine arts and there is no other source of noble works of the fine arts than noble character." It is intriguing to read today that, during a period of ascendant nationalism in Europe, he should have identified race as the source of the aspirations of a society.

Traveling in Europe in 1856, Norton met John Ruskin in Switzerland and formed a friendship that lasted a lifetime, though Norton found Ruskin exasperating and irresponsible. Their walks together in Venice at that time sparked Norton's keen interest in the church of St. Mark, and through it, in medieval architecture. Ruskin's influence on Norton, marked in his *Notes on Travel and Study in Italy* (1860), waned thereafter. Norton, at an earlier time an enthusiast for the work of Palladio, may have learned to hate Renaissance architecture and ornament from Ruskin. But ultimately he came to feel that Ruskin evaded the exacting work of searching out archival and other historical sources and that he understood architecture only in terms of its surface decoration.

In 1874, the recently appointed president of Harvard, Charles W. Eliot, a cousin of Norton, though himself indifferent to the arts, appointed Norton to a professorship created for him, in the history of the arts of construction and design in relation to literature, a title that the candidate had probably proposed. The first classes were disappointingly small, but by 1894, 446 students were enrolled (out of an undergraduate body of 1,925). Initially Norton's lectures were illustrated with drawings and prints of the objects and buildings discussed, but this had to be abandoned as enrollment increased, and works of art had to be discussed without visual images; lantern slides were employed first in 1896. The outline of Norton's course for 1874 lists forty-five lectures, of which almost half were devoted to ancient art. Only one was assigned to Romanesque architecture, with examples from Italy, Germany, and England; the absence of France is astonishing considering that the English Romanesque had been imported from France.

Perhaps the most direct influence of Norton's teaching on the future history of art was through one pupil, Bernard Berenson, who took from the professor his reverence for the enriching and morally elevating potential of art, but whose reputation was based on a refinement of connoisseurship through a method—entirely different from that of Norton—involving intensive examination of individual works of art and the determination of the styles of artists and the communities in which they worked. The mark of Berenson's divergence from Norton's moral and literary treatment of the arts is his creation of the world's richest photographic archive of early Italian painting, now the centerpiece of the library at the Harvard Center for Renaissance Studies, in the villa outside Florence bequeathed by Berenson to the University.

Norton's approach to the arts of the Middle Ages focused on architecture, and is most clearly defined in his *Historical Studies of Church Building in the Middle Ages: Venice, Siena, Florence* (1880). It is a book rich in historical and literary background to the buildings he discusses, in many places illuminated by references to documentary sources and inscriptions; there are no illustrations. Norton ignored the visual experience that could have informed his analysis and given the reader a mental image of the buildings. In over thirty pages on the church of St. Mark in Venice, he traces the sources of the church's style, discusses the materials used, and refers to the decoration of the domes—without describing the mosaic technique or the gold ground that gives them their distinctive character (he focuses on their function in instructing those who could not read the Scriptures). The largest section of the chapter is devoted to the life and works of the Doges who served during the period of construction. Little attention is paid to the role of construction in the realization of architectural form; the technical innovations that brought about Gothic architecture are not explained, nor is the importance of the French contribution. Yet, read as political and social history, the book is impressive for its time.

CHARLES HERBERT MOORE

Charles Herbert Moore (1840–1930) was trained as a landscape painter and in 1871 came to Harvard as instructor in freehand drawing and water color in the Lawrence Scientific School. Three years later, when Charles Eliot Norton was appointed lecturer on the history of the fine arts as connected with literature, he asked Moore to teach a course in Harvard College on principles of design, painting, sculpture, and architecture. Through Norton, Moore met Ruskin while traveling in Europe in 1876–1877, and joined him in Venice. Ruskin enjoyed conversation with Moore, and wrote to Norton that "He is not at all so wicked nor so republican as you, and minds all I say." Moore believed, with Ruskin, that the practice of drawing and painting was essential for the study of the appreciation and history of art, a view that was continued in the Department of Fine Arts from its inception until the retirement of Penman Ross and Arthur Pope half a century ago.

Moore, inspired by the work of Eugene Viollet-le-Duc, soon set out on a career as a scholar of medieval, principally Gothic, architecture, and in 1890 published *The Development and Character of Gothic Architecture*, which he illustrated with his own instructive but drab drawings. The book anticipated the work of Kingsley Porter in locating the source of Gothic vault construction and buttressing in Lombard architecture.

Moore's approach, in marked contrast to Norton's, focused on France and emphasized the importance of building technique in the formation of the Gothic style. He scrupulously avoided reference to such affects of the architecture as light, color, texture, and surface decoration. His focus on the constituent structural elements of Gothic, the vault constructed over ribs and the flying buttress, was formed principally by the writings of Viollet-le-Duc, who was the leading exponent of the Structural school of interpretation, and avoided the broadly humanistic views of Ruskin and Norton, which had emphasized the cultural relevance of architectural elements and ornament.

Moore was appointed the first curator and in the following year director of the Fogg Art Museum, which had been built in 1895. Shortly after, he was promoted to professor of art. On Norton's retirement, Moore took over his celebrated course on the fine arts of the Middle Ages and Renaissance (although Moore also published a book on Renaissance architecture, he had absorbed Ruskin's and Norton's distaste for it, and wrote as if it offended him morally).

On his retirement in 1909, he settled in England in order to continue his work on Gothic architecture, which led to the publication of *The Mediaeval Church Architecture of England* (1912). The book defines English Gothic as derivative of the earlier Norman style imported from France at the time of the conquest, and of the Gothic introduced, also from France, by William of Sens, the designer of Canterbury Cathedral. While he found all of English medieval architecture lacking in structural logic, he allowed that Early English Gothic had a certain beauty. Moore died in England at nearly ninety in 1930.

ARTHUR KINGSLEY PORTER

Arthur Kingsley Porter (1883–1933) came to Harvard as a professor in 1920 (number 41). He studied at Yale as an undergraduate and took courses in the Yale Art School. On graduation, he spent the summer traveling in Europe and was so exhilarated by French medieval architecture that he dropped his plans to study law and enrolled in the architecture school at Columbia University. Returning to Europe in the spring of his first year, he again changed course, deciding to pursue archaeology and the history of art, and he began to work on his first book, *Medieval Architecture: Its Origins and Development* (1909), directed toward students and non-specialists, which was published when he was only 25. Throughout his career he insisted on basing his work on the actual, firsthand experience of buildings and sculptures and not to rely more than necessary on the written word.

He was invited to teach in the school of architecture at Yale, where he stayed for five years. In 1911 Yale University Press published his essay, *The Construction of Lombard and Gothic Vaults*, which proposed the theory, not widely accepted, that the ribbed-vault system basic to the style of Gothic architecture had evolved from earlier eleventh-century North Italian practice, and had been developed in order to avoid the labor and the expense of constructing complete wooden centering in making vaults. His initial Italian study was the foundation for his monumental publication, *Lombard Architecture*, of 1915–1917.

Kingsley Porter was independently wealthy, and in the post-war period, his Harvard appointment stipulated that, in order to have ample time for field work, he should not be bound to regular teaching. His extensive travels in France, where his interest changed to sculpture, led him to his most important publication in 1923, the ten-volume *Romanesque Sculpture of the Pilgrimage Roads* (one volume of text and nine volumes containing 1,525 plates), which, inspired by studies of the medieval epic, broke with the tradition of investigating medieval styles by region to demonstrate that the social–religious phenomenon of pilgrimages from northern Europe to Santiago de Compostela in Spain brought about a community of expression along the pilgrims' routes. The work is extensively illustrated with photographs taken by himself and assistants. In 1922 Porter was instrumental in the acquisition for the Fogg Art Museum of a major group of French Romanesque sculpted capitals from the church of Moutier-St. Jean and five from the church of St. Pons (number 16), which are now are displayed around the museum's court. Later he arranged the purchase of other capitals, as well as the unique wooden *Virgin Annunciate* from Spain, and he himself made gifts of sculptures from the period.

In the late 1920s Kingsley Porter began a long-lasting dialogue with the young Meyer Schapiro—the preeminent scholar of Romanesque art of the next generation—whose dissertation and early publication on the portals the abbey of Saint-Pierre at Moissac and the church of Saint-Martin at Souillac, both in southern France, are in important ways indebted to Porter's approach and discoveries. In 1928 Porter complemented this work with the two-volume *Spanish Romanesque Sculpture*.

He left his huge accumulation of photographic plates and prints, a selection of which is in the exhibition, (numbers 36, 37, 38, 39, and 40) to the Fine Arts Library. At the end of his life, stimulated by his long friendship with the Irish poet and political figure, AE (George William Russell), he became absorbed in Celtic art; his final work was *The Crosses and Culture of Ireland* (1931). He disappeared in 1933 in a storm along the Irish coast, near his grand estate, Glenveagh Castle, Donegal. He and his wife bequeathed to Harvard their Cambridge estate, Longwood (which now serves as the President's residence), a University professorship, and a chair in the humanities.

KENNETH J. CONANT

Kenneth John Conant (1894–1984; number 42), graduated from Harvard College in 1915. He received a graduate degree in architecture in 1919 after serving on active duty in France, and entered practice in the Boston firm of Perry, Shaw and Hepburn. But a return to Europe a few months later, and the start of a close friendship with Arthur Kingsley Porter, led him to abandon design in favor of teaching and research. He was appointed instructor in the Harvard School of Architecture in 1924 and, in the following year, received a Ph.D. in fine arts after writing his dissertation, guided by Kingsley Porter, on the Romanesque pilgrimage church of Santiago de Compostela, to which Porter's study of the art of the pilgrimage routes had conferred special eminence.

Already at this time Conant had discovered the focus of his life work: the excavation and reconstruction of the ruined Abbey of Cluny, Europe's preeminent monastic establishment of the Cluniac Order. The appearance of the abbey, which had been leveled in the French Revolution, could be retrieved only by drawn reconstructions based on extensive excavations of the foundations, and Conant set about learning the techniques of field archaeology at sites in the Yucatán and New Mexico. Digging, which was restricted to pits throughout the site, was complicated by modern building over the ruins, illustrated in Conant's drawing in the exhibition reconstructing the third and substantially larger church built on the site over a photograph of the modern town (number 49). Excavations of the abbey began under the auspices of the Medieval Academy of America in 1928 and continued until 1950. A scientific report was not published, but Conant's extended and well-illustrated description of the results of the campaigns, sponsored by the academy, was published in the town of Mâçon in 1968 with a dedication to Arthur Kingsley Porter (*Cluny: les églises et la maison du chef d'ordre*).

Documents and excavation revealed the appearance of the three successive churches on the site, of which the third (Cluny III) was the largest abbey church in the Christian world. By putting together evidence from the remaining portions with drawings and prints of the complex from pre-revolutionary times, archival documents, and the results of the excavations, Conant was able to provide detailed reconstructions (numbers 44, 45, and 47). Sufficient evidence was uncovered of the form and structure of the preceding church (Cluny II, built 948–981)—three aisles wide in comparison with the later five-aisle construction—to produce a convincing image of an early Romanesque structure that conforms with others of its time (number 43). Remains of the first church, however, the foundation of which documents fix at 927, were obliterated by the later construction, and Conant's conclusions about its design are based on remains of contemporary churches of comparable scale. Conant claimed that the outstanding group of ten capitals from the apse of the third church and fragments from the portals were seminal to the formation of the Romanesque style throughout France; they rank among the finest achievements of Romanesque sculpture (numbers 15 and 48). He constructed a full-scale model of the apse colonnade with casts of the capitals in Warburg Hall of the Fogg Art Museum in the fall of 1933 (number 46).

Conant claimed that Cluny had anticipated many of the characteristic features of the Gothic architecture that was to follow, such as figural sculpture in the door jambs and the flying buttress (the latter hypothesis was not generally accepted).

Although his work on Cluny was a consuming passion throughout his later life, Conant did not engage in original medieval research, though he did publish for the Pelican History of Art series a survey, *Carolingian and Romanesque Architecture, 800 to 1200* (1959), comparable—except for the exclusion of Gothic—to those by Moore and Kingsley Porter. He employed his extraordinary gift for architectural rendering in recording the buildings of the Boston area and in proposing reconstructions of Renaissance buildings (most notably a perspective of St. Peter in the Vatican as seen from the front, according to the unexecuted project of Michelangelo Buonarroti).

ERNST KITZINGER

In more recent times, the distinguished medieval scholar Ernst Kitzinger brought medieval studies eastward to the spheres of Byzantine art, initially at Harvard's Dumbarton Oaks Research Library and Collection in Washington, D.C. where he had been a junior fellow (1941) and fellow (1945). A year later he was appointed to the faculty there and, in the period from 1955 to 1966, served as director of studies, and thus became a mentor of many junior scholars who had come there as fellows and are now teaching throughout the country. On several occasions during his tenure at Dumbarton Oaks he came to Harvard to teach and, in 1967, was named the first Arthur Kingsley Porter University Professor, joining the small group of outstanding scholars appointed by the president outside of the departmental structure. He retired in 1979 and now lives in Oxford and Poughkeepsie, N.Y.

Much of Kitzinger's early work, during his five years as assistant in the British Museum, was devoted to the arts of the Early Middle Ages; his guide of the collections in that field has been important not only for those visiting the museum, but also as an incomparable—and still invaluable—general introduction to the period. In the 1940s he turned to Italy and the Mediterranean littoral, focusing on mosaics in Sicily (*The Mosaics of Monreale*, 1960), North Africa, and Greece. Several of his major studies (on "The Horse and Lion Tapestry at Dumbarton Oaks: A Study in Coptic and Sassannian Textile Design," "The Cult of Images in the Age before Iconoclasm," and "The Hellenistic Heritage in Byzantine Art," were published as long articles in *Dumbarton Oaks Papers*. They illustrate how his work has oscillated between attempts to clarify significant aspects of Byzantine art through the investigation of individual objects—perhaps the legacy of his work at the British Museum—and an application of cultural history and criticism to the basic issues of the period. He is most widely recognized for his masterful overview of Byzantine art, *Byzantine Art in the Making*, published by Harvard University Press in 1977, based on his 1974 Slade lectures at Oxford; the book was characterized by a colleague Irving Lavin as "The fruit of a lifetime of work by one of the most painstaking and innovative art-historians of our time, [the book] is supremely deceptive. It is brief, lightly documented and eminently readable by anyone interested in the history of culture. Yet it is a landmark in art history, for it signifies the end of a chronic tradition in which the period between antiquity and the Middle Ages was regarded as a Decline and Fall.... This is the first time the age has been treated as a whole, with the visual history deeply embedded in its intellectual matrix...."

RECENT SCHOLARSHIP AND TEACHING IN MEDIEVAL ART

One of Kitzinger's pupils at Harvard, Henry Maguire, who is now at Johns Hopkins University, taught in Harvard's Department of Fine Arts from 1973 to 1979. Ioli Kalavrezou, presently the Dumbarton Oaks Professor of Byzantine Art History in Harvard's newly named Department of History of Art and Architecture, was affiliated from 1975 to 1977 with both Dumbarton Oaks and the University of California at Los Angeles. Her work has focused on sculpture (*Byzantine Icons in Steatite*, 1985) and manuscripts (*Images of Legitimacy: The Paris Psalter*, in progress).

Two faculty members whose work focused on the Romanesque period in Western Europe taught at Harvard for extended periods: Linda Seidel (1967–1976), now of the University of Chicago, and Robert Bergman (1976–1981). Seidel's Harvard dissertation on *Romanesque Sculpture From the Cathedral of Saint-Etienne, Toulouse* was published in 1977; she also collaborated during the 1970s with Walter Cahn of Yale on the New England volume of *Romanesque Sculpture in American Collections* (1979). In the course of a thorough study of Kingsley Porter's photographs, she became intrigued by the frequent appearances of equestrian sculptures in the archive, and began research for a book, *Songs of Glory: the Romanesque Façades of Aquitaine* (1981). Bergman's principal focus was on medieval crafts. His book, *The Salerno Ivories: Ars Sacra From Medieval Amalfi* (1980), based on his Princeton dissertation was prepared during his time at Harvard. At the time of his recent untimely death he was director of the Cleveland Museum of Art.

Serafin Moralejo, Fernando de Ayala Professor of Spanish Art at Harvard beginning in 1993, a scholar of early medieval art who has concentrated on Spanish Romanesque sculpture and architecture, returned to Spain at the close of the 1999 academic year. Professor Christine Smith of the Department of Architecture in the Graduate School of Design has been offering advanced courses in medieval and Renaissance architecture that are available to undergraduates and graduates in the Faculty of Arts and Sciences.

Secondary Sources

Fasanelli, James, "Berenson Without Baedeker: Some Notes on His American Sources, *Harvard Library Bulletin*, XVI, 1968, pp. 156–166.

........, Charles Eliot Norton and His Guides: A Study of His Sources. *Journal of Aesthetics and Art Criticism*, 26, 1967, pp. 251–258.

Schaffer, Robert B. *Charles Eliot Norton and Architecture*, Ph.D. dissertation, Harvard, 1951.

Seidel, Linda, "Arthur Kingsley Porter: Life, Legend and Legacy," *Early Years of Art History in the United States*, ed. Craig Hugh Smyth and Peter M. Lukehart, Princeton, 1993, pp. 97–110.

Note: The Harvard University Archives is the source of valuable biographical material on past members of the faculty, and the News Office is a source for information on living members.

I am indebted to Linda Seidel and Christine Kondoleon for observations on the recent history of medieval studies in the Department of the History of Art and Architecture.